Small
Places

Small
PLACES
IN SEARCH OF A
VANISHING
AMERICA

Thomas H. Rawls

LITTLE, BROWN AND COMPANY

Boston   Toronto   London

First Edition

Library of Congress Cataloging-in-Publication Data

Rawls, Thomas H.
    Small places : in search of a vanishing America / Thomas H. Rawls.
  — 1st ed.
      p. cm.
    ISBN 0-316-73482-9
    1. City and town life — United States.   2. United States —
Description and travel — 1981–   3. United States — Social
conditions — 1980–   I. Title.
E169.04.R37   1990
973 — dc20   90-36723

10 9 8 7 6 5 4 3 2

Designed by Barbara Werden
FG

Published simultaneously in Canada
by Little, Brown & Company (Canada) Limited

Printed in the United States of America

To W. W. R.,
the queen of the hop

Contents

Acknowledgments

FIRST, Castle Freeman, a prince among men, who encouraged me to find my voice.

Foremost, to Wistar, who pretends she likes the sound of it.

Also, Albert Wertheim, a special professor; Jack Osander, who showed the way; Craig Canine, a supportive colleague and friend; James L. Lawrence, the founder and publisher of *Harrowsmith*, in which these pieces originally appeared in slightly different form; Alice Lawrence and Wendy Ruopp, of *Harrowsmith*, exacting copy editors.

To all the people who spoke openly with me, and to all those trusting people in small places everywhere who would have if I had asked.

Small
Places

Introduction

PILGRIM IN THE WEEDS

WEEDS — Everywhere the weeds are spreading, displacing native plants. Weeds aren't necessarily just unwanted and ugly plants like crabgrass in the flower garden, diminishing the beauty of a horticultural design; nor are they merely intruders like lamb's-quarter or tumbleweed competing with food crops on our agricultural land, diminishing the economic value of a planting. By weeds, I mean outsiders — plants from somewhere else, be it Europe or Asia or wherever. They are opportunistic, rogues like burdock and thistle that move in where man has disturbed the land. They are without natural controls, and like loosestrife, which is invading the eastern and midwestern marshes, they may be lovely. Weeds, even ordinary ones like plantain, are exotics, and they have remade the landscape. The result is that many areas are now dominated by fewer, similar plants that have outcompeted the distinctive, native species that once occupied special niches.

And what is true in the natural world is true in the human world. Just as the short-grass prairie was made up of particular plants suited to specific conditions, small communities near nowhere in particular were made up of

3

people who stuck close to their hometowns, adapting to the microclimate of their locale. They came to speak with decided accents; their economies traditionally were built around the local resources — the forests for wood and for game, the hillsides for grazing, the flats for crops, the rocks underground for fuel or currency. In many cases they were Third World economies, where raw material was shipped out and manufactured goods were shipped in. The land often yielded a marginal living, and the lean life gave rise to plainspoken people proud of their ability to make a go with what was at hand, which often wasn't much.

The small communities could be insular, inbred, violent; they could be equally warm and generous. Invariably, the most ambitious of residents would in their youth strike out to play in a larger arena, and these small communities were, inevitably, depleted of talent. For the most part, our society didn't pay much attention to the drab, gnarled, fibrous-rooted people who held fast in small places. But then, the weedy riot began.

Some twenty years ago — it is hard to believe it was that long ago — the big city suddenly didn't look so attractive to a lot of people. The metropolis — American society itself — was too crowded, too noisy, too hectic, too mindlessly striving, too technocratic, too dangerous. (For some, too crowded with uncommonly hued weeds, who spoke the language in alien accents.) The unhappy, the disenchanted, the searchers, weeds all, were loosed upon rural America.

In some instances, this sowing was a good thing, some new genes into the shallow pool. Along with the nodding, mumbling dropouts came doctors, teachers, lawyers; novice farmers, down on their knees cultivating, sanctifying the soil; questing, energetic souls looking for a life's work. Many came to small places hoping to find communities where the enduring values of home and craftsmanship and respect for nature remained intact. They arrived with some notion of learning a new way — the old ways — and of fitting in.

Weeds are durable — plantain, to mention but one — and they have tremendous resilience: when was the last time you actually eradicated a dandelion? They can be beautiful — like loosestrife. But like loosestrife and dandelions, when they move in, they tend to take over. And where the human weeds have arrived in numbers, they have sought dominion, and the unique environment of a small place is altered by the new vegetation.

Over time the motivations of the newcomers seemed to change. Both the early transplants and their more recently arrived cousins have become concerned with remaking country places, altering them to be more convenient, more consistent with the neighborhoods of their upbringing. The intention today appears to be to improve small places rather than adapt to them. Increasingly, economic considerations have become more important than spiritual ones. A way of life gives way to making a good living. Perhaps growing up was ever thus, but I feel a terrible sadness about what is happening.

I am a weed, born and raised in Philadelphia, where as a youth I found my pleasure in the upper deck behind first base at Connie Mack Stadium. Now I am, by choice, a resident of a small place in Vermont, a state where there isn't even a minor league baseball team. I arrived here by way of Missouri, Washington, New Jersey, and Wyoming, with other brief stops along the way, another seed carried on the wind. I can take root only where conditions are favorable, but being man, I can change conditions to make them favorable. That is what my kind has done. Blending in a bit, but altering more, sometimes by our mere presence and alien background.

Before this transformation, each individual rural community might have been limited, but in total, these small places offered a rich diversity. With the spread of us weed people, homogeneity between towns is becoming the rule. The sounds of the voices in any one place and even the landscape itself begin to resemble those found in other places.

Viewed another way, it seems that in every small place, one of two things is happening: it is dying or it is being killed. The ones that are dying are the out-of-the-way places that don't offer work — the ground is too infertile even for weeds. And the young men and women flee. A small-town sheriff said it directly: "When you lose your youth, you lose your town."

Many are heartland towns, places out in the middle of the country deeply afflicted by the economic problems that plagued farmers for a decade. Many are places populated in significant measure with older folks, those returning to their childhood homes or retirees simply looking to let their clocks wind down in the sort of quiet town they've always dreamed of. The pace is right — as are the prices. During the earning years, it is no easy matter to scratch up the income needed to survive in one of these unpopular places, but they prove a relatively light touch on the bank account when a fixed income is paying the bills.

The places that are being killed are an entirely different matter — popular beyond reasonable measure, growing, bursting, destroying themselves — overrun by weeds. Many are resort towns, places blessed by a striking natural beauty. These towns in the mountains and on the coasts are metastasizing, the cancer of success spreading, for example, down off the ski slopes into the once-remote villages below. Other doomed towns are those that once were beyond the urban fringe but soon will be no longer.

They are all seeing multitudes of new residents move in. The newcomers have money, and are using it to transform the rural town into a neo-suburb — better schools, paved roads, rising real estate values and property taxes to match. The next generation of natives can't afford to live in their hometowns. Their parents are selling out (resentful but glad for the check) or making good money as a backhoe operator or carpenter (resentful but glad for the check) or ending up in the servant class, mowing lawns, say, or serving meals (resentful, diminished, and unimpressed with the check).

I like the poor places. They have a down-at-the-heels look, the architecture is commonplace, the food in the local eateries is greasy, but the people are friendly and pretense is dealt with firmly. Such communities remain most distinctive, most genuine; they successfully hold on, perhaps paradoxically because of their failure to attract attention, to the things that made them what they always were.

In the prospering places insidious forces are at work, and that saddens me. You can see that these communities were once everything a body ever could have wanted in a hometown, with dramatic natural surroundings and often with handsome buildings as well. But they have been caught in the pernicious grip of fashion — which is to say, they are blind to pretense — and they are becoming parodies of the things that originally made them so special.

For the past dozen years I have worked as an editor of two different magazines devoted to country life, magazines largely read by us weed people. Over that time I have been witness to developments in my own communities and in those that are far away. Out of simple curiosity I decided to drop in on a variety of different places, starting a few years ago. And as someone who has governed most of his life on the basis of a hopeful, doglike instinct, I just followed my nose in finding them. I heard of a platinum mine and thought I'd have a look. I knew about the cold in northern Minnesota and decided to feel it for myself. An acquaintance told me Point Reyes, California, was beautiful; another said that Osceola, Missouri, got a raw deal, and I figured, being a pilgrim, I would visit the shrines. I learned of two journalists trying their hand at farming — their story was irresistible to me, who in the abstract envied them their life. I had always wanted to discover what made the Amish tick, never mind the woolly-headed stuff about their quilts, and I figured everybody ought to see Alaska once. I did not seek out these places to make a formal study, to demonstrate any individual point, or develop any central thesis. I just went out and poked around and talked to ordinary people, in the belief that every place and every person has a story to tell. Then I came home and tried to write their stories.

Someone — George Orwell, I believe — wrote that there are two reasons to write: to show off and to report unpleasant facts. I won't comment on the first half of his equation, but I would suggest that the quirky, the individualistic details are more representative of everyday life than the disagreeable ones, and I would suggest that he forgot to mention the third reason to write: to tell the truth as you see it. I am trying to be honest about fifteen places I was lucky enough to happen upon, offering my impressions. I hope it can be said that I have not only described accurately these small places as I found them, but that I have revealed in some small way what lies at the heart of each.

Chapter 1

THE EYES OF GOD

GRINNELL, IOWA — What Cheer, Hawkeye, Early, Morning Sun, Belle Plaine, Charter Oak, Red Oak, Oakland, Walnut, Lone Tree, Forest City, Little Sioux, Sioux Center, Sioux Rapids, Ute, Cherokee, Pocahontas, Elkhorn, Eagle Grove, Coon Rapids, Shell Rock, Marble Rock, Rockford, Lime Springs, Grand River, Riverside, Gladbrook, Mount Pleasant, Greenfield, Pleasantville, Clearfield, Vail, Nevada, Washington, Wyoming, New Virginia, Holstein, Schleswig, Correctionville, Diagonal, Gravity, Independence, Manly, Defiance.

There is poetry on the map of Iowa. The landscape is a song, an uncomplicated tune of clear whole notes rolling within an octave or two of each other. But for some, the lyrics suggest an elegy, the music sounds like a requiem. This is hurting country, and many here are already mournful.

Corn is down. Beans, meaning soy, are down. Land prices are down. Hogs are up, though — you can see them snorkeling through the corn stubble in the spring — and that helps. The question seems to be: Who is going to survive? Which farmers? What towns? And just what is it that we are losing?

10

I am standing on the corner of Fourth and Broad, turning slowly and generally gawking, entirely unaware that before me stands an architectural landmark, a bank designed by Louis H. Sullivan, the man Frank Lloyd Wright called "the master." As I rotate slack-jawed and, apparently, befuddled-looking, a kindly woman inquires, "You look confused. Can I help you?" "Oh, uh, no, thank you," I reply, because however confused I appear, I am no more puzzled than is normal for me. I am just taking in the scenery, wondering if I can absorb some small bit of this town, thereby sparing myself the necessity of having to rely entirely on reason to figure out what makes it especially Grinnell. Then, as I amble up Broad Street on an unseasonably warm spring day, the first two people I pass on the sidewalk smile and say, "Hello." They do not merely nod or mutter an unintelligible greeting; they offer a genuine, articulated salutation. Perhaps it is the warm spring weather. Perhaps knowing everything about everybody else in town, they save their good wishes for strangers. But I doubt it.

They are friendly. They are open. They want to help.

Welcome to Grinnell. What can we do so we will not someday have to mourn its passing?

"Go west, young man." Horace Greeley, the famous editor of the New York *Tribune*, is reputed to have offered that celebrated counsel to Josiah B. Grinnell, a thirty-two-year-old Congregational minister from Vermont. Grinnell took it. With three friends, he bought 6,000 acres in the American midlands and in 1854 founded a new town. Five years later, he moved Iowa College — which is now Grinnell College — from Davenport. John Brown, the abolitionist, was a welcome visitor here. Alcohol was not. When J. B. Grinnell sold off lots in town, they were accompanied by covenants forbidding in perpetuity the consumption of alcohol on the premises.

In Grinnell's founding, one finds the sturdy triangulation that has trussed up small-town America for more than a century: education (the college), opportunity (a land of unbroken sod, with its topsoil measured in feet, not inches), and religion. The religion, by whatever name, was a dissenting religion, what the author Tom Wolfe calls a "proto-revolt against the aristocracy." Wolfe developed his theory about the influence of religion on small-town America in an article on Robert Noyce published in *Esquire*. Noyce is perhaps Grinnell's most celebrated son, more so than even J. B. himself. The son of a Congregational minister, Noyce grew up in town and went to college here. A decade later and half a continent to the west, he invented the integrated circuit made of silicon, the tiny chip upon which the modern computer industry is built, leading Wolfe to remark, "Every high roller in Silicon Valley comes from a small town." What is it about these towns?

Today, on a spring evening in Iowa, Wolfe is expounding his theory in Herrick Chapel on Grinnell's campus at a college-sponsored symposium on small-town America. A dandy, dressed in a white suit and black-and-white shoes, the author of *The Right Stuff* struts his own. He is an entertainer and a provocateur. As Wolfe talks on, faithful listeners sit for more than an hour on the uncushioned wooden benches of the chapel. Perhaps Wolfe wants to give them a tangible feel for, hard evidence of, the discipline required of J. B.'s original flock.

Discussing how small towns were shaped by the dissenting Protestants — the Methodists, Presbyterians, Baptists,
and others — Wolfe summarizes their radical, democratic
theology: "God does not reside in an official church body.
God is the light shining in the eyes of every human soul.
God is running hither and thither in every human breast."
This is revolutionary stuff. The doctrine meant that every
man was, as Wolfe puts it, "a secular saint," who was not
bound by class but had a chance to improve his lot.

J. B. himself led the way. His worldly success was to be
seen not merely as a measure of his adherence to the Protestant work ethic, which, according to Wolfe, is usually
"translated glibly to mean an ethos of hard work and self-
denial." No, J. B.'s success was a measure of his devoutness,
and his uncommon devoutness — "the internalized eyes of
God" — drove him to his material success.

Material success and devotion can still be found at Fourth
and Broad. The architect Louis Sullivan's renowned Pow-
eshiek County National Bank stands on the northwest corner. It is a temple — literally. Behind the tellers is an array
of ten tall stained-glass windows; in each is the repeated
image of a crucifixion. Christ died for your sins, and as his
eyes shine down on you, while you enjoy the feel of those
crisp new bills, the light of God in you is revealed in your
success. God and Mammon are married. There is an internal
contradiction in this union — some call it hypocrisy.

One of the legacies of J. B. Grinnell and his dissenting
brethren is the widely held view of small towns as places of
false piety, gossip, narrowness, and materialism. Those are
indeed characteristics of small-town life — and, by the way,
of power centers like Washington, D.C., and of money

centers like New York City — but these characteristics are no more than the flip side of all the virtues that are embedded in the character of small towns: religious conviction and self-discipline, concern for your fellow man, sense of community and the need to work for the common good, and — The Dream — a chance to make a good buck.

Sharp Lannom is wearing a gray suit. Most days he comes to work in shirt-sleeves, but today he is dressed up for his appearance as the moderator of a panel that is part of the symposium on small towns being held at the college several blocks away. The topic: "The Small Town and American Enterprise." Sharp Lannom is an enterprising man.

He took over DeLong Sportswear, the family business, twenty-five years ago, when he was twenty-two years old. The company, which is descended from the oldest manufacturing business in continuous operation west of the Mississippi, has nine manufacturing plants besides the one in Grinnell, employing a total of 1,300 people nationwide. "We believe in small plants in small towns," Lannom says. "That allows the plant manager to know the people who work there. What you get in a small town is the work ethic, the determination to do a good job."

Your high-school letter jacket, which has probably survived all the years since you graduated, might well have been made by a diligent small-town laborer in a DeLong plant, as might the softball uniforms in which the local team of aging, pinguid ballplayers adorn themselves. Lannom says there is no profit to be made in uniforms for professionals. "We try to avoid making things at a loss. We consider it un-American." DeLong is aggressive, like the athletes it outfits. "We're cuttin' up the competition pretty good."

Grinnell itself is more than holding its own. A town of 8,900, including students, it is buffered somewhat from the agricultural depression by the presence of J. B.'s college, with its 1,250 students, 500 employees, and $210 million endowment. (If you are wondering whether the college is near downtown Grinnell or near the edge of town, consider the explanation of one resident: "One corner of the college is near the downtown, and one corner is near the edge of town.") Other substantial nonfarm businesses that provide the town with an economic foundation for the future include the Midwest headquarters of GTE, Grinnell Mutual Reinsurance, and Miracle Recreation Equipment, to cite a few. But for local agricultural enterprises like Gold Sun Feeds, Farmhand, and small DeKalb and Cargill facilities, not to mention the farmers all around, the future is uncertain, at best.

There is also uncertainty, at best, for the oil-patch towns of the Southwest, as for the major industrial centers of the North. Our national economy is in transition — the world economy is being transformed. Economically, we are squatting in a hut in the global village, and just as auto workers in Detroit must compete with car builders in Japan, corn farmers in Iowa have to compete with grain producers in Latin America.

Thomas C. McRae, president of the Winthrop Rockefeller Foundation in Little Rock, Arkansas, which is a leader in small-scale economic development for rural areas, says of small towns: "If we're simply trying to preserve the old without understanding what the opportunities are for the future, we're all going to be left behind. I think that in an economy of transition, there's incredible opportunity for rural America."

The old is spoken of with nostalgia. The old is a five-cent cup of coffee, which is, in fact, still available in Grinnell — it seems as though Grinnellians tout this curiosity as if to say, see, things haven't changed here. The old is stability, knowing your neighbors and knowing they will be there tomorrow. The old is knowing the diversity of storekeepers along Main Street and patronizing them (not slipping out along the highway to the absentee-owned Wal-Mart conglomerate, a pernicious invader that can undersell the competition in town; the Wal-Mart founder, Sam Walton, has made himself one of the richest men in America, and his multibillions have come out of the pockets of small businesses on Main Street in the heartland). The old is family farms, where a man could make an honest and decent living, raise a proper family, and have a place of value to pass on to his children.

The old — if we can call something that dates back to the fifties old — is also monocultural commodity-crop farming, the hedgerows 'dozed out and vast acreages planted to corn and beans and, farther west, wheat. It is a food-growing culture that was predicated on cheap oil — for cheap fertilizer, cheap pesticides, and cheap transportation. At the grocery store, we got cheap food and were pleased and asked no questions. And in the heartland, where the little towns are dotted, the monocultural farming was a part of the old monocultural economy: agriculture.

"While the roller coaster was going up, no one had to plan ahead," Sharp Lannom says. In 1985, however, with the joyride in a steep descent and people's stomachs in their throats, some of the leaders in Grinnell took action. They launched "Grinnell 2000." A nonprofit foundation, it would look to the future, to see the opportunities that emerge in the transitional times. "It would be a catalyst to make it possible for the community to become what it desires for itself," according to Ben Webb, the foundation's executive director. Grinnell 2000 was launched with the idea that it would be a "grass roots" organization, providing anyone the chance to have a say in Grinnell's future, to have a hand in imparting some design to his or her town. Presumably people choose to live in small places in order to have that influence over their lives — or, put another way, they like living in small places because the forces that shape their lives don't seem so overwhelming. If, however, you are suffering because of the general downturn in agricultural fortunes, because, say, overseas markets have been lost as a consequence of the stormy geopolitical climate, it is probably difficult not to feel like a speck of dust caught in a fierce wind. Nonetheless, by looking ahead, the foundation hopes to help people to understand and direct the forces that would shape the town rather than have people passively react to whatever weather blows their way.

"Economic development has to be everyone's business!" Tom McRae of the Winthrop Rockefeller Foundation exclaims. "Development occurs when local residents invest their personal savings and their talent and energies to accelerate economic development."

One of the gathering forces Grinnell, like other small towns, will have to prepare for is the aging of the population. In fifteen years, Iowa will have one of the highest percentages of nonworking elderly per capita of any state. The old folks, many of whom left with bright visions and grand desires as youths, will return home. "It's like a reunion," Sharp Lannom says. It is a gathering that could strain the town's ability to provide health care, that could mean a shrinkage in numbers of school-age children and a consequent erosion of support for education. The aging trend, not surprisingly, could lead to a reduced work force locally. How is Grinnell — and how are small towns everywhere — going to stay vital and pay for the aging of their populace?

According to Grinnell 2000 projections, the town will have to grow to about 12,000 to remain vigorous. "In order to provide the robust economy that we want to have as working people, we cannot stay stagnant in numbers of people," Lannom says. "We have to attract a diverse mix of industry."

Diversity means stability, a truth that applies to nature, to agriculture, to investment portfolios, and to small-town business communities. One of the great dangers of the retail chains is that they diminish diversity: one store can supply what formerly required many. (Their second shortcoming, and one not to be taken lightly, is that their ownership — the equity — is not local, and their profits are not reinvested in the community. Which is to say, they are mercenaries.)

People everywhere agree on the importance of diversifying their local economies, of attracting new industry into their towns. Thomas McRae has strong views on the subject. He is a long, thin man with a friendly drawl. Get him out of his dark suit and let those bony wrists hang from shirtsleeves an inch too short, and you've got yourself the picture of a country boy. Despite McRae's languid speech, small towns eager for new employers would be wisely schooled if they were to listen to him:

"The Fortune 500's employment in this country is not growing. The people who want to recruit firms to states like Iowa should understand we are going to lose industrial jobs faster than we can replace them with new plant locations. The kindest thing I can say about a state policy based primarily on industrial recruitment is that it's moribund.

"In today's economy, most new jobs come from small business. Fewer than one in a hundred new jobs come from relocation of plants from out of state, and yet the tax incentives, the industrial incentives all go to assist the industrialist who is locating from out of state. Small business is discriminated against. The state's industrial incentives are not used to help expansions of home-grown industry."

Calling tax subsidies for business nothing more than "welfare," McRae remarks, "All you have to do is go before the legislature and say, 'This is good for economic development,' and they will roll over and give it away. One of the most unseemly cases of prostitution that I had noted in a long time was the tremendous wiggling and maneuvering that states went through to get the Saturn automobile plant." McRae is referring to the interstate competition to court General Motors. Spring Hill, Tennessee, was the successful suitor. Will there be a happy marriage or did this little town in central Tennessee just import some big-city social diseases?

As Sharp Lannom suggests, the trick is not simply to attract new industry to town, to expand and prosper; the trick is to do that without altering the essential character of the town. "I still want to be among people who know me, to be able to cash a check anywhere in town."

McRae's solution is to "build a local economy." He explains, "We have to begin to look at and understand how local economies work. What do you import? What do you export? What are your natural resources? A small college in Arkansas recently did a study to determine where their food came from. Arkansas is the largest producer of fryers in the United States, but the poultry consumed at that school came from North Carolina. Arkansas is the leading rice producer in the country, but the rice came from Texas and California. Some of the beef did come from Arkansas, but it was fattened in west Texas and slaughtered in Chicago. It's incredible to me that a state like Arkansas, an agricultural state, imports one-point-two billion dollars' worth of goods a year, nearly eighty percent of what it eats. There are some million-dollar businesses there somewhere.

"And that's where the opportunity lies if we are going to begin to take advantage of what's going on locally. We have to understand our strengths. We have to build on them. How do we add value? How do we keep dollars at home? If you view your local economy as a bucket with a lot of holes in it — every time you send dollars out, they're gone forever. You can keep them here and turn them over a couple times — there's a multiplier effect."

The girl selling me a bottle of pop has a total of nine rings and studs in her left ear. This is the sort of decorative mutilation one grew up seeing in the photographs of aboriginal tribeswomen featured in *National Geographic*. Despite the changes in their packaging over the years, small-town youths remain the object of unalloyed affection. Here at the symposium, held at an institution dedicated to the flowering of youth, speaker after speaker offers the experience of his or her small-town youth as a model of what growing up ought to be. Sharp Lannom says of his boyhood in Grinnell, "People cared about me not so much for what I was, but what I could become."

Boys and girls grow up in a mingling of rich and poor, in a place where to make things work, people must participate. They move among adults who know them, and they learn what it takes to earn their respect. The adults watch with those internalized eyes of God that shaped the midwestern Protestants, and the youths feel the demanding eyes of the Lord on them, and in their turn they internalize the message, disciplining the raw self and attuning it to mesh with society. As Grinnell's favorite son, the inventor Robert Noyce, says, "You can't cut people off at a stop sign. They know you. Therefore you are more careful about treating fellow human beings as fellow human beings."

Thomas McRae was among the many speakers in Herrick Chapel who noted that small towns have produced a disproportionate share of leaders. "The biggest bank in the state of Arkansas has a national advisory board of corporate CEO's of major U.S. corporations. It's said that when that group assembles and all are present, there is more than eighty-five billion dollars of gross national product assembled in the that room. All of that group, save one, were from tiny Arkansas towns, half of which don't even exist anymore." McRae then asks the inevitable question: "Well, what is it? Why should people, so many of whom came from small towns, have been so successful?"

His answer: "When you grow up in a small town, you can see how everything works. To survive you don't have to specialize or focus on one aspect of life. You can take a step back, and you can understand the whole system." That understanding usually means the ambitious kid is going to leave town. Like less-developed communities the world over, small towns suffer from a brain drain.

If you have to give up your best, though, you cannot help but be left with a sense of failure, which Paul Gruchow calls "one of the central themes of small-town life." A bashful, bearded man recently turned forty, Gruchow was a successful small-town newspaperman in Minnesota who turned himself into an admired book author. Speaking at the symposium, he says, "There is an assumption in every small town by every person who's there that if you're there, something must be wrong with you. Bill Holm, a writer, says, 'You know, nobody came to Minneota, Minnesota, who had been a success somewhere else.' Nobody did, really, let's be honest. We believe this to the point where we don't even know when we're insulting each other about it."

Gruchow then relates an anecdote. A local boy has been implicated in a murder in another state. People in his own town, Worthington, knowing the kind of boy he is, are convinced he is innocent. They want to find him a good lawyer. As it happens, Gruchow's wife is a criminal defense attorney. One night Gruchow gets a call from a fellow citizen concerned about the boy, asking if he, Gruchow, can recommend a good lawyer — *in Minneapolis*. The request was made with no thought that it might be insulting to Gruchow and his wife. The assumption was simply that no top-flight attorney would choose to practice in Worthington.

Then Gruchow, who has chosen to live in a small town, goes on to elaborate on this idea of our deep-seated, unexamined belief in the second-rateness of our small-town neighbors, of our belief in our own inferiority: "I recognize this in myself. My accountant is in Minneapolis. My own attorney lives in the Twin Cities. Whenever my children have had surgery, they have not had it, I guarantee you, at the local hospital, which is a regional medical center. This is part and parcel of our lives."

A small town is a place caught in a dilemma. In some ways — economically, professionally — it aspires to be a bigger place; socially, it wants to stay small and intimate. If it succeeds economically, offers top-flight professional opportunities, it may keep its sons and daughters, but then it will not longer be, in essence, a small town.

What is that essence? "Everybody minds everybody else's business." The speaker is Richard Lingeman, raised in Crawfordsville, Indiana, which you probably have not heard of, and now an editor in New York City, which you have. The qualities of caring and conforming implied in Lingeman's remark have proven themselves to be nurturing to youth, who almost inevitably — to their credit — break the bonds. To many, the exodus of young talent is a reason for lamentation. To others, it is a source of pride. Ultimately, they say, well-formed youth is a small town's greatest export.

If small towns were no more than wellsprings of fresh talent, they would deserve our attention for that attribute alone. But they are more, and besides, like people, they are significant in their own right, not simply for what they have achieved. Grinnell is one of thousands of ordinary towns in which men and women proceed on their daily journeys — breathing, eating, loving, earning a living, and perhaps by chance accomplishing something that might be called progress. But let us not get too enchanted with progress, rather let us cherish those places where people breathe and eat and love.

Chapter 2

THE LIGHT OF GOD SHINES FORTH

ANTELOPE, OREGON — The land here is spare. It is not the Oregon of great timber stands, of plentiful rainfall and lush growth. Oregon east of the Cascades is first cousin to desert, actually is desert in some places, with rough hills of volcanic rock. Here in the southern part of Wasco County, at 2,500 feet above sea level, the native vegetation runs to rabbit brush, juniper, and bunch grass. Twenty years ago, when Margaret Hill was planning to move to Antelope from Montana to take a teaching job at the local school, her seven-year-old daughter explained to friends, "We're moving out in the weeds."

Some fifteen years later, Bhagwan moved in too. Bhagwan was Bhagwan Shree Rajneesh, the recently deceased, iconoclastic Indian guru with a gift for attracting wealthy adherents and a taste for fine cars — Rolls-Royces, to be precise — fancy watches, and sex. Worldwide at the height of his glory, Bhagwan's followers were said to number in the hundreds of thousands, and in the early and mid-eighties, some 4,000 disciples — called *sannyasins* — from around the globe joined him and the rattlesnakes amid the volcanic outcroppings in the hills nineteen miles east of town. Bhagwan — you do not say "The Bhagwan" any more than you would say "The Jesus" — moved onto the Big Muddy Ranch, 64,229 acres, where he lapsed into a self-imposed silence of three years' duration while his adherents went to work, spending between $100 to $200 million building a New Age Vatican.

In backwaters everywhere, townsfolk worry — with reason — about the influence of new residents, how the outsiders want to change things. It used to be, in small towns, that endurance was power, and that natives would simply outlast new arrivals, who brought with them the latest fashions in government and education, but left when life got monotonous or the weather got cold. In Antelope, however, the townspeople found themselves contending not merely with a few new arrivals, but with thousands of Rajneeshees, people who looked human enough, but dressed and acted like no humans they had ever met or would ever hope to see again. In Antelope, every small town's fears grew to hallucinatory proportions.

People in Wasco County tell you that if the Rajneeshees had simply minded their own business, everyone could have gotten along fine. Most everyone who lived in Antelope was there by choice. Many were retired, and their business, such as it was, was to enjoy the outdoor life, hunting for deer, pheasant, and chukar, and fishing on the Deschutes and John Day rivers. Much of this country is dedicated to ranching, a difficult business where water is so scarce, but the calves grow up on the sere hills. People hereabouts are proud of what they have and could understand why others would want to move in and enjoy the local blessings. The influx of a large group of outsiders is unsettling, but still, you mind your business, we'll mind ours.

The Rajneeshees' fundamental business was spiritual. They were making the journey inward, seeking the true self. Mostly white, average age in their mid-thirties, married, and college-educated, the Rajneeshees came from all over the world. They were trying to escape whatever traps they had fallen into in earlier, conventional phases of existence. They sought to start life fresh. "Most people go for what somebody else wants, not what they want," explained Anuradha, a handsome, poised forty-two-year-old Englishwoman who was president of the Rajneesh Neo-Sannyas International Commune. ("Yes, I teach you selfishness," Bhagwan said.) At Bhagwan's command, they clothed themselves in the colors of the sunrise, as an emblem of their new lives. "We're crazy, you know," said Maneesha, a devoted follower. "We're in this to transform ourselves as individuals."

That was the inner business. The external business was to transform an overgrazed stretch of arid high country into a city where the journey inward could be pursued in peace.

But the new arrivals never did get to mind their own business. Whether that is because they didn't want to or weren't allowed to is a snarl that will never be untangled. What is certain is that the Rajneeshees developed the Big Muddy's agricultural land into a city, the better to supply such necessary services as telephones, sewage treatment, and roads. The 1000 Friends of Oregon, a nonprofit state-wide land-use organization, quickly filed a lawsuit against the incorporation of the city of Rajneeshpuram. The watchdog group charged that the city violated state land-use laws. Perhaps, as the plaintiffs professed, the development represented a dangerous precedent in a state with strong land-use laws — or perhaps the Rajneeshees found themselves with legal problems simply because they were too alien to be trusted as neighbors. (Almost two years later, the Oregon state attorney general filed a lawsuit challenging the incorporation, arguing that it violated the constitutional requirement for the separation of church and state.) Suspicion bred conflict, conflict bred hatred. The Rajneeshees, who had seemingly limitless assets, decided to play by their own rules. When they were thwarted in creating their own town, they literally bought one that was already lying around. They acquired property in the nearest available place, which happened to be Antelope. The faithful moved in, the Rajneeshees having concluded that the sure path to victory was to stuff the voting districts rather than merely the ballot box. The long-time residents, sensing a takeover, attempted to thwart the Rajneeshees by trying to disincorporate Antelope and turn its administration over to the county. The gambit failed, though, with the Rajneeshees now being in the majority. They proceeded to elect their own red-clad kind to the Antelope city council and begin to run things — pulling off a pseudodemocratic coup. To make the invasion — and the insult — complete, the newcomers renamed the town Rajneesh.

By and large the Rajneeshees were unapologetic about their takeover. "People have a right to control their environment," argues Sarita, who handled press relations for the Rajneeshees. Hers is a true and fair sentiment, insofar as it goes. It just doesn't go so far as to acknowledge the rights of the people who were in Antelope to begin with. In Sarita's personal history, one discovers the story of the underdog triumphant, baring its teeth in success. Perhaps her story is in important ways the story of the collective Rajneeshees in Antelope.

Sarita grew up unhappy, but her parents gave her what she calls "an incomparable jewel — my freedom." At fifteen, she was in New York studying dance, when an interest in Indian dance took her on an overland pilgrimage from Europe to the promised land. There she met "The Ultimate Dance Master" — Bhagwan. She became a devoted follower.

Sarita tells a story of how, after returning to the United States, she and two companions moved into a small town in northern California. They did not fit in particularly well, and one night, shots were fired outside the house in which she was living. Taking the gunplay as a warning, she and her friends moved away the next morning. Sarita knows what it is like to be an outsider, to be unwelcome and powerless — and she knows what it is like to be run out of town.

So when she and several thousand fellow sannyasins found a remote spot to settle down in, they could not be bullied. "We were threatening to the people of Antelope," she admits, but, on the basis of her earlier experience, she believes, "if we had been a small group, they would have run us out." Because the Rajneeshees arrived in force, however, Sarita says they were able to give an impromptu civics lesson: "The people in Antelope learned what it is to be an American. Small, rural communities forget." Forget, that is, according to Sarita, that everyone is not like themselves and that the majority rules, even a new majority, even a majority that is buying its way in.

What money can buy — the external business:

- Let's start with the Big Muddy Ranch, renamed Rancho Rajneesh, 120 square miles of land for $6 million.
- Add 94 Rolls-Royces for Bhagwan to take his daily drive in.
- Big D-8 bulldozers and smaller Bobcats; front-end loaders; tractors; airplanes, and an airport with a 4,500-foot-long paved landing strip; hundreds of trucks, vans, and cars; 109 yellow buses for public transportation by Rajneesh Buddhafield Transportation.
- Mirdad, the visitors' center and Chamber of Commerce. Like all visitors, I was required to check in here before being allowed access to the ranch. Also I had to sign three forms releasing various Rajneesh corporations from any liability if I were harmed, even if as a result of gross negligence on their parts. In addition I signed a form consenting to be searched at any time I was on the ranch. This requisite penmanship was done under the gaze of several closed-circuit cameras. It was also here that I registered for the hotel, getting a pink plastic bracelet, like a hospital patient's. And it was here that I met Sarita. A small, trim woman with full lips, prominent nose, and long dark hair, she was, like all Rajneeshees, wearing a *mala,* the Rajneesh rosary: a long necklace with wooden beads and a wooden oval framing Bhagwan's picture. On the day I met her, Sarita's sunrise garb consisted of a pink cotton jumpsuit and hot-pink, down-filled boots. Needless to say, the red garb of the commune-ists seemed all too appropriate to many outside the ranch.

- A chain of eateries — restaurant, pizzeria, ice-cream parlor, snack bar, and deli — all named Zorba the Buddha, after the model man: sensual like the Greek, spiritual like the Asian.
- Hotel ("luxurious," according to the literature), with 140 (bugged) rooms. Provided in the bathrooms were free safe-sex kits, condoms and rubber gloves, to prevent the spread of AIDS. (Bhagwan was quoted as claiming that he had had more sexual partners than anyone in history. "People who are disciples of Bhagwan live much more naturally than most people, who have been repressed," Sarita says, although disciples say the sexual activities of sannyasins have been exaggerated. "People everywhere are doing it, but people here are honest, open, frank," Sarita says.) The television in the room had one working channel — with videotapes of Bhagwan saying, "I'm not like Jesus, proclaiming himself as being the son of God — and all that crap." (Laughter from his followers, who delight in Bhagwan's humor and rebelliousness.) And following one of his typical long pauses: "Don't be bothered by inconsistencies and contradictions. Tomorrow this day will be old, gone. . . . Be always in the present, and you will be always right." I stayed in room #31, named Acceptance: "Nothing is good, nothing is bad, all is divine."
- Krishnamurti Lake (after the Indian philosopher), 44 acres of surface, holding 330 million gallons of water. The impoundment, used for swimming and irrigation, was created by Gurdjieff Dam (after the

Russian mystic), 300,000 cubic yards of fill in a dam
400 feet long by 90 feet high.

- An innovative, diversified farming operation —
  scorned by the local ranching and farming
  traditionalists. It included deerproof fencing for some
  50 acres of fertile bottomland along the John Day
  River; four propane-heated greenhouses (one 180
  feet long) and plastic tunnels and movable frames to
  cover several acres of vegetables; a dairy; an 8-acre
  orchard and 10-acre Omar Khayyam vineyard, and
  1,900 acres in a dryland grain rotation. Also beef
  cattle. What were vegetarians doing raising animals
  for slaughter? some wondered. (Don't be bothered
  by contradictions, Bhagwan said.) In addition,
  everywhere along the eroded banks of the Big
  Muddy, the creek running through the ranch, they
  planted trees.
- Housing for the hardworking sannyasins, the Lao
  Tzu townhouses and the Mohammed and Jesus
  trailer parks. Vast sums of money were spent, but
  this spiritual city in the desert didn't spring forth
  without teeming sannyasin laborers. For the
  Rajneeshees, work is worship, as though in their all-
  embracing, blenderized spirituality, they made room
  for the Protestant work ethic — with its material
  rewards.
- Rajneesh Mandir, a two-acre meeting hall for
  meditation.
- The Rajneesh International Meditation University,
  where the basic search to find one's true self was
  pursued. The central Rajneesh quest is to shed

outside influences — the values and self-repression
demanded by others — and therapies were
developed by Rajneeshees with experience in
Rolfing, postural integration, primal therapy,
bioenergetics, Zen meditation, vipassana meditation,
and more. As might be expected, a considerable
portion of Bhagwan's followers have formal training
in psychology. In Rajneeshpuram, life was an
extended therapy session.

Margaret and Phil Hill live in a one-story bungalow with
yellow vinyl siding, which offers one of the few bits of color
in this otherwise drab, defeated-looking town. Next to the
walk leading to the house is a silver queen maple, on which
is tacked a sign: No TRESSPASSING. Inside, the house is perfectly kept: the sheet music on the piano is tidy; no ashes
dust the raised hearth of the fireplace.

Phil Hill, nearing the Social Security years, is wearing
plain brown pull-on boots, blue jeans, and a blue chamois
shirt. Like many of Antelope's residents who predate the
Rajneeshees, he is retired, having spent twenty-three years
working on the county roads. Margaret Hill is a trim, neatly
dressed woman, with glasses, graying hair, and a slightly
downturned mouth. She was the mayor of Antelope at the
time of the invasion. It was not easy to be the head of a city
under attack by alien forces.

Only twelve people were living in Antelope when I visited, eight of them pre-Rajneesh. Houses sat empty along
the streets, and adding to the desolation were the barracks
from a mining camp the Rajneeshees had brought in for
housing. Some had been put in place, but others sat unfin-

ished in the schoolyard, and more were perched on cinder blocks, like discarded mobile homes, in the vacant lot across from the Hills.

In that same lot, a member of the Rajneesh security force used to stand, sometimes all day, watching the Hills house, sometimes taking pictures if the Hills walked out, sometimes just watching. Just standing and watching.

After the Rajneeshees gained control of the Antelope city council, they contracted with Rajneeshpuram for services. Antelope had no taxes, but when Antelope became Rajneesh, it got a tax assessment of $20 per $1,000 in valuation. Many residents on fixed incomes could not afford that. In addition to having no control over their taxes, the original residents were confronted with a further grim, outraging indignity: their tax money went to Rajneeshpuram to provide police "protection." As a result, the original residents of Antelope helped underwrite Bhagwan's private security force. As Margaret Hill said, "We were in effect paying for our own harassment."

In her capacity as mayor, Margaret Hill was involved in eleven different legal actions with the Rajneeshees during one four-month span. There were disputes over water rights for a printing plant the Rajneeshees wanted to build, conflicts over building permits, and challenges about the way the Antelope city council did business. (Hill and her son eventually responded by suing the day-to-day leader of the Rajneeshees for defamation.) Margaret Hill mentioned the ordeal of one deposition she had to give in Portland, four hours away. She was questioned for eight hours. Many of the suits never came to trial, but Phil said, "Those lawsuits drain you and drain you and drain you . . ."

". . . of time, money, and emotion," Margaret finished.

The strain of coping with the Rajneeshees embittered the Hills. Shadings of meaning have given way to understanding only in black and white. The experience has, in some cases, driven a wedge between neighbors and families — if you weren't against the Rajneeshees, then you must be for them. The Hills and their neighbors looked for help from various officials, but, to their minds, it was slow to come. Feeling the absolute truth of her view, Margaret Hill wanted the government to respond quickly and decisively, but the fact is, democracy is a messy, unwieldy operation, and our judiciary gives everyone who asks for it — even the member of a cult — his day in court.

The post office in Antelope, zip code 97001, is a remodeled mobile home with new mailboxes. Outside, a red rooster and a gray chicken forage in the driveway. Inside, Bill Dixon, postmaster, attends to his duties. He is a rough-hewn man whose granchildren are the fifth generation of Dixons in the area. He and his wife used to live in town, but they moved to the family ranch nearby. "I wasn't a redneck before," Dixon says. "But I am now."

When you follow Bhagwan, Maneesha said, "Get ready to experiment with life." The experiment at Rajneeshpuram was, however, done under extraordinarily restrictive circumstances. The paradox of cults is that they free their followers from the repressions and unhappiness of the past — "Disciples have *deprogrammed* themselves from society," Sarita commented — but cults demand of their disciples close adherence to a new standard. It is the paradox of any convert, who gets to shed old beliefs, dead values, and false truths in return for embracing a new system usually every bit as demanding and rigorous as the one discarded. The convert does not free himself from authority; he merely pays homage to a different one.

Rajneeshpuram was spiritual boot camp. Rajneeshees took a new name, a new uniform, and were surrounded by like-minded others. They lived in barracks. Outsiders were given only limited access. The loudspeakers around town broadcast Bhagwan's teachings; the newspaper reported on Bhagwan and his disciples.

The conventional view in our society holds that it is one thing to take our business seriously. That is good, and it brings prosperity. It is proper to take our families seriously. That is honorable. It is fine to be religious — grace at dinner, church on Sunday, that sort of thing. But to take religion seriously, actually to be guided by religious conviction: that is a bit much, a sign of a troubled spirit. Therein lies unreliability. And to take psychology — what Jung called the religion of the modern era — too seriously. Therein lurks disturbance. All this probing of psychic legacies and the emotional temperature-taking of the self-improvement crowd: what an unseemly business!

Could those who are content to play their assigned parts live at peace with an unconventional, radical crowd who genuinely believed they could, to paraphrase from another time and another place, find the light of God that shines within them?

At 7:45 A.M., the sun is coming over the hills, hitting the fencing wire. Frost makes sequins of the barbs. The school bus heads west on the county road from Antelope to Madras, and, along the road, ranchers are feeding their cattle. Normally Derald McCall, foreman of Roy Forman's Indian Creek Ranch six miles west of town, would have been feeding, but at the moment, he is getting his health back after being thrown while breaking Tuck, a 1,500-pound red sorrel quarter horse. "We like a big horse for the rough country, and Derald doesn't usually get boiled," Roy Foreman says. But the back cinch on Derald's saddle broke, and he pitched forward onto his head, crushing three vertebrae in his upper back. When the ambulance came to get him, his rescuers didn't want to risk driving him out over the bumpy ground, so they called in a helicopter from Bend, sixty miles to the south.

In his early forties, Derald is a slender man, about six feet tall, with sideburns that run long. At one end of the front room of the family's small house on the Forman ranch hangs a portrait of John Wayne against an imaginary western landscape. At the other end of the room is a big Northern Comfort wood stove, made nearby in Madras. Derald gets cedar logs by the truckload on the Warm Springs Indian Reservation. He has been foreman at the Indian Creek Ranch for going on a decade, and although he admits he would like to have his own ranch, he is careful, he says, "to treat this one just like it's mine."

The Indian Creek Ranch is 10,000 acres of deeded land, another 10,000, give or take, of leased land. They run almost 2,300 cows, mostly black baldies (Angus-Hereford crosses), and 54 bulls. They take about 200 tons of hay off 100 irrigated acres and grow some oats and barley. Additional feed is bought, including 500 tons of bluegrass screen-

ings — hulls, straw, broken seed — from the seed farms
around Madras. (In neighboring Jefferson County, some
9,000 acres are planted to grasses for the lawn-seed industry
and 12,000 acres to peppermint — more than in any other
county in the United States.)

The Forman ranch, after the annual cycle of calving and
branding in the spring, haying in the summer, gathering
stock and weaning calves in the fall, has been able to sell its
calves for about twenty cents a pound less than the cost of
raising them. A 400-pound calf, which is typical, loses $80.

One year Derald helped make up the loss by digging up
a massive petrified sequoia log on the ranch. They sold some
50,000 pounds of twelve-million-year-old wood. The deal-
ers get about seventy-five cents a pound, so petrified wood
isn't a bad crop to have. Derald has also run a trap line,
catching bobcat and coyotes, which, he says, "are more of
a problem than people realize."

He does not seem too concerned, though. Derald doesn't
strike one as a man who gets riled up about things. He was
president of the Antelope school board when the Rajneeshees moved in, and he had his hands full. They would
show up en masse for a meeting and shout Derald down.
"They'd get real nasty" is all Derald says about it. He got
calls at all hours almost every night. "It was a type of harassment, I guess," he comments. In his official capacity on
the school board, he was sued . . . how many times? He
asks his wife, Caroline, who remembers exactly: four times.
None came to trial.

The school wasn't anything grand — grades one through
six, with five children the year the McCalls moved in, up to
maybe as many as fifteen one year. After elementary school,

the kids rode the bus to Madras. Derald finally resigned one September, on Caroline's birthday, and all the local parents arranged for their youngsters to go to Madras for elementary school too.

After the Rajneeshees took control, the locals did not want to send their kids to school in Antelope for what, to Derald, are obvious reasons: "They were a sex cult." Besides, he adds: "I heard that they had no desks, just rugs and davenports. The kids just lay around on the plush rugs."

A man does have his pride, though, and Derald had a response, of sorts, to the situation. "I'd put my rifles in my gun rack and drive into town and just park. They didn't know what to do," he says in a slightly defiant tone. "We harassed them too," he adds, but his voice trails off, as though he were overtaken by embarrassment at the admission. Derald is a valuable man on a ranch. He is a good mechanic: "I can make anything run, just about," he says. And Roy Forman called him "one of the better ranch riders around." He is also quiet, not given to expressiveness, but I sensed that he did not want to be seen as a patsy.

Roy Forman thinks matters with the Rajneeshees were overblown, an attitude that has lost him friends. Pushing seventy, a broad man with a hobbling walk and a hearing aid, he doesn't seem concerned. He can remember rougher times: "There was less violence than we used to have at Saturday night dances."

One day, I stopped at the cafe at Willowdale, a few miles outside of Antelope and visited with Caroline McCall, who works there. Did anyone ever jump a Rajneeshee? I asked. No, she replied. The sign in town was shot up, but there are fools everywhere who take signs to be fair game. No, the so-called rednecks never rolled a redcoat. Caroline squared her shoulders: "That's one thing we're real proud of. It proved we're not what they said we are."

Unbeknown to the greater population of sannyasins, a cadre of Rajneeshees ultimately resorted to illegality in an attempt to maintain their hold on their small piece of eastern Oregon. They flaunted their weapons, but secretly introduced salmonella into salad bars in The Dalles, the county seat to the north, and conspired against county officials. Members of the ruling clique fled, and eventually several were convicted of a variety of felonies. Bhagwan, "Blessed One," was whisked back to India, having pleaded guilty to violations of immigration laws. His Rolls-Royces were sold. The Big Muddy Ranch, reborn as the City of Rajneeshpuram, was put on the block.

Ravi Dasa, a slight man with thinning hair, wire-rimmed glasses, and a beard giving way to gray, was once a physician. After seven years, being a doctor was "eclipsed." This day he was dismantling the greenhouses, removing the lights.

Inside the greenhouse, flats of lettuce were coming along; peas and sunflower seeds were germinating, but they wouldn't mature. Going back and forth from greenhouse to pickup, Ravi Dasa, in brown coveralls, toted lights. Was he sad? "No, it's what I'm doing now."

"This town is dead," proclaimed one Rajneeshee, a handsome, bearded young man with a German accent. Soon he would be moving on, but for the moment, he was serving up bran muffins and expensive fruit juices at the Zorba the

Buddha coffee shop in Antelope. A Rajneeshee couple on their way down the road to Boulder, Colorado, came in to say good-bye. Hugs all around, a scene that was repeated many times as the commune emptied.

Where can a cult go today? The Massachusetts coast was spoken for early in the 1600s. The Mormon polygamists found safe harbor on the shores of the Great Salt Lake. Is there any real estate still available?

In the end, the Rajneeshees began to disperse, many southward, toward warmth. Rajneeshpuram, an odd hybrid, more enduring than an annual but not a true perennial, grew and blossomed; it became a fat seedpod, and it burst, and the seeds were flung every which way by the unpredictable, uncontrollable energy that propels people to remake themselves. All over the world, little patches of aspirants garbed in the sunrise will try to take root again.

For the Hills and their neighbors, the worst of the ordeal is over. Now that the town is back in the hands of genuine townspeople, they aren't being charged for irrigation water in the summer, so they can grow a garden again. "We can grow most anything except tomatoes," Margaret Hill says. Still, in a querulous voice, she adds, "Nothing will give us back those years. We were a community that was open and trusting. Now we're wary, skeptical — bitter, a lot of us."

Over at the post office, Bill Dixon is feistier. Having been able to move out of town during the Rajneeshee occupation, he does not seem to have been so consumed by the Rajneeshee swarm. He has even considered returning to Antelope. "The reds are gone. This town'll come back," he says, "no doubt about it."

Chapter 3

THE SCALDED FROG

MOUNT HOPE, OHIO — Rebecca Hostetler* has lived up to her reputation as an Amish cook. Whenever the neighboring farmers pitch in at the Hostetler farm, they know that Rebecca's dinner will more than repay them for any calories spent working in the field. Eli Yoder and I helped Samuel Hostetler get in the last of his corn this forenoon, and Rebecca is making sure we have enough fuel to carry us through until supper.

Following a minute of silent prayer, we tuck in. There are meat loaf and scalloped potatoes, green beans in cream sauce, and coleslaw elaborated with bits of cauliflower, along with cottage cheese and homebaked bread. Rebecca has cooked enough for five, because orginally Eli's son and

* All of the Amish with whom I spoke asked that I not include their names in this book, so I have made up names. Since a number of Amish family names like Hostetler, Yoder, Miller, Fisher, and Troyer, to mention a few, are extremely common, it is possible, even likely, that the names I have given to the people I spoke with are the actual names of Amish living in various settlements around the United States. No one should think, however, that those individuals were so vain as to want their names to appear in print.

a neighbor were going to help with the field work and join us for dinner. They had to cancel and have left Eli and me to labor mightily at the table. We are too polite to leave any serving dishes overly full as an insult to the cook. Then comes dessert, layer cake and peaches in syrup. Having done my manly duty, I am stuffed as a tick.

But lurking over on the corner of the table sits an untouched pecan pie. To my alarm, it appears that the pie, also, is a part of this meal. Eli, sizing up the situation, says that he would enjoy a sliver of pecan pie and tactfully suggests that I split a piece with him. I agree. We eat our pie, and Rebecca's honor is upheld. Ours too. The meal ended, we bow our heads and offer a silent prayer of thanks.

Eli Yoder and Samuel Hostetler are farmers in their early forties. They live within a mile of each other and operate typical Amish farms here in Holmes County, which is in the middle of the largest settlement of Amish anywhere in the United States. The farms and houses are close to narrow gravel roads, along which the Amish travel by horse and buggy. It takes a moment to realize why this rolling landscape is different from similar scenes elsewhere, then the reason comes clear. There are no power lines or telephone lines running along the road or cutting across the fields. Having become so acclimated to overhead lines, we do not consciously take note of them, but when they are not there, the view opens up and the landscape looks the way it should.

There are 15,000 to 18,000 Amish in east central Ohio, precise figures being impossible to obtain, in part because the most conservative, or low, Amish, called Swartzentrubers, refuse to let anyone count them. All Amish do not take such a reclusive stance. Occasionally a small wooden shed can be seen sitting by the side of the road; it houses a communal Amish phone. Phones in Amish country suggest all is not static in the dooryards of the Plain People. No doubt the Amish must always struggle to limit outside influences, but in what has essentially been a farming community, not all Amish sons are able to go into farms. Life here is not so simple, sheltered, immutable, or free of the stresses of the outside world as postcard images would lead one to believe. The Amish strive to remain a farming people, because a community of family farms allows their religious convictions fullest expression. Yet in many ways, some ingenious, the Amish are adapting to, and compromising because of, the coming of the twenty-first century.

To see the process by which Samuel Hostetler's feed corn gets picked and husked, you would not think a whole lot of adaptation had taken place. Samuel has hitched a team of Belgian mares to a flatbed wagon. Eli and I ride with him to the field where some 35 shocks of corn still stand. The individual stalks, still holding their ears, have been cut by hand and tied into small bundles, and the bundles have been laid up into teepeelike shocks, bound by baler twine. Eli and I walk along beside the wagon, cutting shocks open and throwing bundles up to Samuel, who piles them on the wagon. The team of horses seems to know what to do without much reining from Samuel. About eight shocks make a wagon load. With the flatbed piled high, we head back to the barn, where the old Rosenthal husker/shredder is cranked into action — to fix the year when this particular machine was made might require carbon dating.

Samuel climbs onto a platform in front of the mouth of

the machine, into which he feeds the stalks that Eli and I hand to him, a bundle at a time. Seeing Samuel so close to the rude chewing of the machine, which is entirely without safety shields, brings to mind the one-armed Amishman I saw the previous day. The antique machine proceeds by the clamorous and mysterious workings of its innards to perform three tasks: it husks the ears, which will be fed to stock, and conveys them into a gravity wagon; it blows chopped stalks, which will be used as bedding for cows, into a thirty-foot-high pile in a corner of the barn; and, being a thrifty machine, in keeping with its thrifty owner, it bags the individual kernels that, predictably, get shaken loose in all the rumbling and clatter.

Except for its noise, this scene contains the essence of Amish farming: neighbor helping neighbor; sturdy horses, capable of producing their own replacements, providing the power, and old machinery kept in working order long after the "English" — as the German Swiss–derived Amish call others — have moved to newer, more sophisticated gear.

The Rosenthal itself is, however, powered by a thirty-foot belt run off a decidedly un-Amish machine: an International Harvester farm tractor. And the wagon into which the shucked corn falls is hitched to yet another tractor: Eli's John Deere. Everyone knows that the Amish do not farm with tractors, yet Samuel Hostetler, who is by no means a progressive Amishman, who still milks his cows by hand and cools his milk in old-fashioned cans, has two such machines, one his own, at his disposal this day.

Much about Amish life and beliefs is revealed in the Amish's limited use of tractors. Amish will use tractor-powered belts to run various attachments. For example, Eli still hooks up his "thrashing machine" — this stationary grain thresher — and his feed grinder to his John Deere. The Amish use horses for all their field work, though. There is one simple reason for the continuation of that practice, as Eli explains: "With horses, you're limited."

He adds: "With a tractor, they have lights. You can plow day and night — if you're crazy enough to do it." With a tractor, Eli, who has 75 tillable acres, could easily plow more than the 30 he turned last year. With a tractor, he could plow Samuel's acreage. With a tractor, Eli could take over Samuel's entire farm, instead of riding a bicycle down the road merely to help him get in the last of his corn. With a field tractor, in fact, he would have a machine that could take him down the road called Progress, and, like many English farmers in Ohio, he might soon arrive at the intersection with Trouble.

An Amish farmer writing about technologically advanced agriculture for a Mennonite publication addresses this issue: "Several years ago in late winter, following a week of unseasonably warm weather, our neighbor to the south couldn't resist the urge any longer and started plowing. I wasn't aware of it until, while walking to the barn, I suddenly caught the aroma of newly turned earth. I stood there, closed my eyes and reveled in it. The promise of spring.

"With [modern equipment] I would have the means to farm his 50 tillable acres, and he could be 'free' to work off the farm. I know I wouldn't be able to do the excellent work he is doing, and I would miss the rich fragrance of his fertile soil. And more than that, I would miss my neighbor."

*   *   *

The idea of *community* lies at the heart of Amish culture, and what one discovers is that for the Amish, unlike most people, daily life and religious life are one. "Our faith and our culture are inseparable," Eli says.

The Amish sect broke off from the Mennonites, with whom they share eighteen articles of faith; the splintering occurred in 1693. Both groups are Anabaptists, which means they practice adult (as opposed to infant) baptism as a rite of church membership. Consequently, the Amish are, as one of their publications put it, "an adult brotherhood of voluntary believers."

Abraham Miller is an Amish minister. He is also a farmer, because all Amish preachers are laymen. They are chosen by lot after a primary vote of the congregation to narrow the field of potential candidates. A sturdy, handsome man with a reddish beard, he is tying up corn shocks as he discourses on his faith. Miller moves unhurriedly, tying shocks and explaining what it means for an individual to be baptized into the Amish church. "He is submitting," Miller says. "There is a dying of himself, and he renounces Satan and the world."

Most people talk of finding themselves, and much of modern psychotherapy is built on the patient's quest for his true self. For the Amish, the goal is just the opposite, as Miller explains: "New birth is the losing of oneself into the greater body of the church, which is Christ's body."

Brotherly love, pacifism, the renunciation of worldliness, and separation from the world are fundamental tenets of the Amish faith, which is simultaneously a gentle faith, but a demanding one. Among themselves, the Amish speak a Swiss-German dialect, and there is a German term that captures the spirit of one who joins the church; it is *Gelassenheit*, which Miller translates as "obedience, humility, submission, and contentment." (Eli Yoder uses the term *yieldedness* to express *Gelassenheit*. "People look at us as though we sacrifice our individuality, and we do surrender, but we maintain our identity.")

Miller goes on to say in his deep accented voice, "A real Amishman will not say he is saved." Indeed, the idea that a mortal could know that he has been saved seems the height of arrogance to the Amish, and in their view, to focus on the precise moment of salvation is wrongheaded. Making a virtue of being saved suggests that being "born again" is an accomplishment, which to Amish thinking denies the fundamental notion of humility. As one Amishman remarked disapprovingly of reborn fundamentalists, "Once they announce they're born again, they usually try to move right up the ladder, I say."

To the Amish what counts is not merely entrance into the fold, but the way a Christian acts. "It is not so much what we claim to be, but what we actually are," Miller says. What the Amish are is expressed in their plain dress. "By the fruit, you shall know the tree," Eli Yoder says. Each church, made up of some thirty families who come together for worship in houses and barns, decides what is allowed by way of dress. Fifteen years ago, no Amishman would wear double-knits — too much the fashion. Today many will, but not the unbending, long-bearded Swartzentrubers. To hold up their pants, Amish men wear suspenders — no gaudy belt buckles for them. Although Amish girls may wear colored dresses, the married women's garments are always dark, muted, and they are done up with straight pins. (How is it possible to fasten a dress only with pins and not poke oneself? I wondered. "I don't want you to look real close at the Amish women," Miller warned me.) Buttons are too showy to be allowed on jackets, but not on shirts, and snaps on jackets are allowed by some churches, but not zippers.

For most of us, putting our legs into a pair of pants and hitching them up is not an act of religious significance. For the Amish, it is. They establish their relationship to God and to the rest of the world with their plain attire — in it, they express their humility, their contentment with God, and their separateness from the rest of us. Lines must be drawn, and as with most man-made boundaries, certain lines can seem arbitrary. The Amish intention is not to dance on the head of a sartorial pin in deciding matters of dress; the intention is to hold their people together. To dress in the latest fashion, to dress in an individual style is obviously a form of self-expression, and often a sign of vanity. Vain people make proud people, and peacocks in fancy, eye-catching clothing would set themselves apart from others in the community, raise themselves above the flock. Such behavior would undermine the church. So in the struggle against worldliness, in submitting to God's will, zippers are out. It is not the zipper per se that is the central issue — what is crucial is that one's attire not distinguish him from his fellows.

Eli Yoder compares the Amish to wheat or grapes: "The individual kernels are ground; the grapes are pressed. After pressing you can never find a single grape. This is somewhat the Amish community."

It is important for the Amish that their outward appearance bear witness to their submission to God, that an individual not stand alone. "Once you stop seeing the face of

God in your neighbor," Eli says, "then you lose community."

Eli Yoder rides in the car with me to a small cheese-making plant outside Mount Hope, which is supplied with milk by Amish farmers. We watch briefly while a young cheese-maker works over three 300-gallon vats. As we tour the storeroom with wheels of cheddar set up to age on the shelves, Eli tells me, "Beer drinkers like sharp cheese."

Being aware that the Amish abstain, I ask, "How do you know?"

"I was told," Eli answers. "The Amish like cheese mild," he continues.

"Why?"

"We don't drink beer," Eli responds, smiling.

We step outside the cheese factory and find my rental car listing badly, a tire having gone flat. Under the hood, I find one of those pathetic, undersized spares that come with cars today. Eli and I put it on, but he is palpably troubled. Finally, he cannot contain himself as he stares at the mounted, temporary spare, eyeing it like a four-inch perch on a stringer hung with fat-bellied bass: "I'd be ashamed to drive with something like that," he says.

I pick up the flat tire and turn it, looking for the source of the leak. Finding a nail embedded in the tire, I pull it out. I present it to Eli. "Looks like an Amish nail to me," I chide him.

"Yeah, it does look like one," he says, chuckling. "It's well made."

*   *   *

Darkness comes early, and the kerosene lamp in Eli Yoder's barn is burning as the family finishes up the evening milking. Esther, Eli's wife, attaches the milking machine to the last of the nineteen cows, all but two of which are Jerseys. Eli's preference for Jerseys is unusual among dairy farmers, both Amish and English. They give less milk per cow than Holsteins, but they require less feed and their milk is higher in butterfat and protein. As a result, the cheese factory to which Eli sells his milk pays him a premium for it.

Much of the young stock belongs to the Yoder children; there are five. Eli and Esther give each child a heifer when the child turns ten. The heifer and her increase belong to the child, while Eli and Esther pocket the milk check. With a bit of luck, each child will have a tidy endowment when the times comes to leave home. David, eighteen, the oldest and baptized into the faith last summer, has had a run of bad luck: his heifers show a penchant for throwing bull calves. Sarah, fifteen, however, has been blessed with heifer calves. Amanda's first heifer is scheduled to freshen soon.

At the moment, Amanda is feeding the hogs, having finished with the chickens, and David is beginning to sweep up. The youngest child, Mary, wearing a green woolen cap that bears a distinctly un-Amish sentiment, "AgriKing, Key to Profit," carries a small bucket of milk to the bulk tank. Matthew, the fourth child, keeps to himself following a dispute with his older brother over the proper way to shoot a bow and arrow. Sarah, hobbled recently when a horse kicked her, is limping inside this evening, preparing supper.

Eli milks his cows with a McCormick-Deering bottle milker. "My vet told me that when I'm done with it, he wants it for his antique collection," he says cheerily. The machine is run by an ingenious system of hydraulic pumps and motors. "The Amish have found hydraulics dependable," Eli reports. In modern milking parlors, the vacuum of the milking machine draws the milk into a pipeline, which then runs directly into a refrigerated storage tank, called a bulk tank. In Eli's setup, the vacuum draws the milk from each cow into a large stainless-steel bottle. The milk from the bottle milker is then poured by hand into a stainless-steel bucket, which Eli, Esther, or one of the children carries to the milk house. "Pipelines are too modern," Eli says. "Christians can carry milk." The milk is poured into a bulk tank, which is cooled by a diesel-powered compressor. The diesel engine also runs an alternator, which charges a battery, which provides enough electricity to run the agitator motor in the bulk tank — to prevent the cream from separating — and to light one bare bulb in the milk house.

Because the Amish limit their use of tractors and because they do not have cars, electricity, or telephones, they are often thought of as being backward. As the workings of the Yoder milking parlor suggest, however, the Amish are not uncomfortable with technology or blindly opposed to it. Indeed, the technology they employ is well suited to their operations.

Some skeptics have questioned these elaborate devisings, created to work within the church ban on the use of electricity. If electricity is bad, why are technological substitutions allowed? And if stand-alone diesel and hydraulic power are acceptable, why not just plug into the grid?

The Amish sometimes ask themselves such questions also, as they refine what arrangements are to be allowed and what is to remain forbidden. Some churches come up with different answers — Eli's friend Samuel belongs to a church that does not permit the use of vacuum milkers, no matter how ancient and how much labor they still demand.

As the kittens finish lapping at their bowl in the corner of the barn, and Eli, ducking his head to avoid the kerosene lamp, carries the last bucket of rich Jersey milk to the bulk tank, it seems clear that a good reason for these distinctly, if seemingly inconsistent, Amish improvisations exists. It may be found in what I have witnessed in the combined efforts of the Yoders on a dark and chilly evening: the cohesiveness of the Amish family.

The Amish make two vows in their lifetime — the first upon baptism, the second at marriage. Both are holy vows, one directly to God, the other before God. We live in a world where promises made before God are routinely broken, but it would be foolish and shortsighted to underestimate the significance of what it means for a genuine believer to solemnly give his word to his god. Nothing is more important than the marriage vow, and consequently, nothing is more important than the family.

Eli Yoder is sitting in the kitchen at the oak table sipping a cup of coffee. The gas lamp overhead glows brightly. On the wall next to him, a large sheet of posterboard is tacked up; on it is a list of the 152 species of birds the Yoders have seen so far this year, including 20 kinds of warblers, a marbled godwit, and a glossy ibis. In the living room, Amanda is reading *The Wizard of Oz*, and Sarah's book is Sterling North's *Captured by the Mohawks*. Mary curls in Esther's lap.

"People have the idea that if you don't have electricity, you're archaic," Eli says. "But I don't feel we're making sacrifices." The Amish do not believe that electricity and the telephone are in themselves sinful, but it is the connections they provide to the world that give the Amish pause. As Eli says, "It's the danger that comes from technology, the temptation it brings," that causes the Amish to avoid it.

As a farmer and as an Amishman, Eli has not fallen into what he views as the trap that has caused so many English farmers to get into trouble. That trap is the belief that a contemporary way of life necessarily offers more rewards and pleasures than those offered within a traditional rural community. "The American attitude toward farming is the dumb son stays on the farm," Eli says. "The smart one goes off to the city to make something of himself."

Eli dares an intimacy: "I had dreams, but I feel if I were to leave this life, I would founder in a sea of ambiguity." A pacifist, like all Amish, he spent two years in Cleveland doing alternative service in a hospital during the Vietnam war; he has been reading a copy of a 1977 University of Chicago Ph.D. thesis about Amish rites; he has taken his family to agricultural seminars in Kansas and canoeing in Minnesota. Eli Yoder may be an unschooled man, but he is not an unaware one. Eli chose not to take that plunge into swirling waters of ambiguity.

For the moment, it is quiet. The gas lamp hisses. In the next room, with Mary nodding off, Esther sings quietly. Eli says gently, "Rocking babies is one of the pleasures of life."

Working with one's family on a farm may be the Amish ideal, but there is only so much farmland in existing Amish communities; consequently a number of Amish have taken to operating cottage industries, like making mattresses. The father can stay at home and work with his sons as they grow up; mothers and daughters can contribute. Many of the businesses are directly related to Amish farming practices — the making of wagons or hames or rope. Andy Troyer makes twisted rope. "Rope Andy," as his friends now call him, would be happy to sell you a twisted nylon tow rope with a breaking strength that exceeds 60,000 pounds. He can sell you polypropylene twists either as short halters or on 600-foot spools.

To make the long ropes, Andy, an ebullient man with a ready, high-pitched laugh, has devised a rope-twisting machine. To buy one would have cost him $60,000; he made his for $1,000. It is run by a two-horsepower Honda engine rigged to a General Motors truck transmission. Rope Andy makes five-eighths-inch rope in third gear, half-inch rope in fourth. "I can make ten spools of rope on a tank of gas," Andy says. "This is a machine what I call elegant."

The Amish culture does not produce artists, the egotism and self-expression inherent in artistry being antithetical to Amish values. The culture does, however, produce much clever machinery. The Amish, like working-class country people everywhere, channel their imaginative efforts toward engineering, not art, toward practicality, not dreams.

Not every Amishman has an idea like Andy's or a banker to back him up. For them, as for anyone who just plain needs a job, there is always the factory, even though working for a conglomerate is hardly the preferred Amish way. In the center of Mount Hope is the Wayne Dalton plant. It does about $60 million worth of business a year making garage doors and is part of a $100 million corporation, the second largest maker of these doors in the nation. About two thirds of the firm's 275 employees are Amish, according to Jack Fisher, a sixty-one-year-old Amishman who has been with the company almost since its founding thirty years ago. Many at the plant, including farmers' sons, work on the assembly line.

"We sort of frown on it," Fisher says of a young Amishman going to work in an English factory, "but you have to adjust a certain amount." Except for a trimmed Amish-style beard, Fisher looks — and sounds — like any small-town Rotarian. "A man has to make a living."

Fisher, like the other Amish who live some distance from the factory, rides in a company van to work every day. Most of the Amish have come to rely on the car, van, and pickup truck, but still they will not own one.

At the Mount Hope auction (held every Wednesday to sell everything from bags of popping corn and homemade noodles to heifers and hogs), eighty-nine horse-drawn conveyances were hitched to the rail that encircles the parking lot. While the Amish arrived in buggies, their livestock mostly arrived in hired trucks. Why rely on the English? I ask Abraham Miller, the minister. Why not allow farmers to have a truck for moving stock?

"What about Amish contractors?" he asks me in reply. "The Amishman who makes mattresses, he must make deliveries. Where do you draw the line? It is easier just to say no. We do hire drivers. A lot of English rely solely on the Amish for their livelihood. To some, it doesn't make sense, but we think it can be controlled a lot better by having not-ownership than by having ownership."

He then cites the example of the Beachy Amish, an offshoot of the faith that allows its members to own and drive cars. (The Beachy are not considered Amish by more conservative orders.) "Originally, it was only black cars and three years old. It was trouble to control, and sometimes a new car is a better buy. And then, what's the difference between a black car and a green car? The grass is green; the trees are green.

"It becomes more difficult to have a discipline than to say no," he concludes wisely.

Allowing cars would add other complications, as Miller notes: "With the auto, the next thing is insurance. We have our own — I don't have enough English, how do you say? — mutual aid. We want to keep our own self-support."

So there is the clarity of the Amish ideal, and the fuzziness of everyday practice. A number of Amish have found that taking an English business partner is one way to remain technically within the church's regulations. An Englishman can, of course, have electricity and phones, and in running a business, these are convenient tools, to say the least. Indeed, an English partner appears to be the perfect way to circumvent the church: some miles to the south, one Amishman rents office space from his brother, who chose to be baptized Mennonite.

Perhaps the Amish face their greatest dilemma in the shortage of farmland locally. Imagine a farmer with one farm and two sons, like Eli Yoder. If he bequeaths the farm to David, what would he pass on to Matthew?

To the south of Mount Hope, the hills tend to be steeper, and many are underlaid with coal. Emmanuel Mullet was raised in an Amish family, but he was baptized Mennonite. He is a rich man, with a major interest in the door factory. He got his start mining coal, including Amish coal. He paid well, and in some cases, he paid with land, two farms without coal for one farm with. A generous price for a farmer with several sons.

So some Amish, who shun electricity and the worldly temptations it makes possible, sold their land to Mullet — some would say, sold out. For a price, they allowed the land to be stripped of high-sulfur coal, which the utilities use to generate electricity. The Amish chose to be separate; it has never been their way to tie themselves to the mast of purity so the worldly English could be freed of the temptation to sin. After being strip-mined, the land is reclaimed, and at a glance the reclamation appears successful. The ground relieved of its carbonaceous burden rolls gently and the grass grows green. An Amishman, a partner of Mullet's, admits, though, that reclamation is not without shortcomings. "It's true, the land is not as good farmland afterwards. But in ten years, you wouldn't know the difference."

This view stirs passion in other Amishmen, who tend to be cautious about revealing much of themselves when in the presence of the English. One farmer who has no coal under his land says that he wishes he did. He is opposed to the strip-mining and would be glad to have his convictions tested. He says of the miners, "I've heard them say they put the land back nicer than it was originally. They think they can improve on God."

He adds sadly, in recognition of how all men can fall short of being their best selves: "We Amish have always considered ourselves the quiet on the land."

To sum up the Amish dilemma, their need to stay separate while making accommodations with the encroaching world, Eli Yoder tells me the parable of the bullfrog. If you drop a bullfrog in scalding water, it will struggle wildly for a moment, then die. If, however, you put that same bullfrog in cool water and then gently turn on the heat under the water, the frog will be perfectly content. As the water gradually warms, the frog will adapt and learn to enjoy it. Then, one moment, without knowing it was ever in danger, the frog dies.

Chapter 4

FRIEND OF THE TREES

CHELAN, WASHINGTON — "Trees are my bag," Skeeter says.

Skeeter is Michael Pilarski, who in 1978 founded Friends of the Trees, "a loosely knit network at best," in Skeeter's words, dedicated to the "Re-Greening of the Earth." Skeeter's great passion is plant life, and, inspired by work of the renowned English forester Richard St. Barbe Baker, Skeeter decided, "You have to plant trees to save the world."

Initially that view seems simplistic and quirky, but Skeeter is eager to make a case for his vision. For example: driving along on the outskirts of Chelan proper, Skeeter pulls up to an intersection. Growing on one corner is a shrub, and Skeeter, brisk and purposeful as a naturalist on a field trip, starts a brief speech. "That's an Oregon grape (*Mahonia aquifolium*)," — Skeeter invariably gives the Latin name when he identifies a plant. — "I've picked from that bush and made jam from the berries."

"Was it good?" I ask. "I mixed it with other fruit to make it better," he answers. "It's also an ornamental, has drought tolerance, and its root is medicinal," he goes on. "It's a source of dye — both the berry and the flowers. Not to mention that it makes oxygen and stabilizes the soil."

He concludes by sketching the big picture: "The world is so degenerated that all the carbon that has been tied up in vegetation has been released into the atmosphere. To tie up that carbon as biomass, we need to plant trees."

St. Barbe Baker, a man whom Skeeter often cites, certainly thought trees were the answer: after studying on the prairies of western Canada, he urged the planting of shelterbelts to prevent soil erosion; he proposed the reclamation of the Sahara by encircling it with a greenbelt of trees that would gradually take over the desert; he was active in saving redwoods in California. And back in 1922, while working in Kenya, he started the Men of the Trees, a worldwide organization that still exists and is, to an extent, the model for Skeeter's efforts.

Skeeter is not, however, a forester in the classic sense that St. Barbe Baker was. He will not be heading off to Nigeria to manage the mahogany forests, for example. Skeeter is a self-taught botanist and, to use his own term, a "networker," operating on the edges of society. He was involved in the founding of Tilth, an organization dedicated to small-scale organic agriculture in the Pacific Northwest. He was the driving force behind the annual Okanogan Barter Fair, which at the peak of the back-to-the-land movement drew some 6,000 traders and celebrants to the Okanogan Valley of northern Washington. Now Skeeter is working as a "catalyst to help people find the information, ideas, and sources they need to get trees planted in their areas." To that end, he puts out an eighty-page newsprint yearbook with the slogan "Think Globally, Plant Locally."

The desertification of the globe — the loss of plant

cover — is a well-documented fact. India and China are suffering from it; so too are Australia and much of Africa. The rain forests in the Pacific are surrendering to the onslaught of the saw. Today, mahogany desks and graceful furnishings with rosewood inlays are clear examples of the maxim that to arrive at elegance one must pass through the gates of wantonness. We will have our style, even if the climate goes to hell.

And in Central and South America, the forests are being consumed by the same appetite that has given us the spare desertlike conditions that prevail through much of the American West: our hunger for meat. Huge tracts of Amazonian forests are being cut over and converted to grazing land. The thin soil wears out quickly, and the ranchers move on. The beef, which is cheaper than U.S. meat, goes to fast-food joints, canned and frozen meat products, and pet food.

Skeeter was a friend of the trees long before everyone else was lamenting the destruction of the rainforest and worrying about the warming of the planet. However global his perspective, though, his arena is local. Ever since he established Friends of the Trees, he has operated an annual spring tree sale. He gets a deal on a remarkable variety of stock from various nurseries in the Northwest, and then he loads up a truck and trailer and peddles his wares for one day each in some four or five towns in central and north central Washington, which has been his base of operations for almost fifteen years. Skeeter estimates that in nine annual tree sales, he has sold some 50,000 trees, shrubs, and vines: red astrachan apple, Jersey blueberry, Nanking cherry, Niagara grape, Oregon champion gooseberry, Manchurian plum, Chinese chestnut, Barcelona filbert, Russian walnut, Russian mulberry, Russian olive, Siberian pea shrub, Scotch pine, Chinese wisteria, American persimmon — to mention a few.

Skeeter also has collected and sold native seeds, a business that he has incorporated into a new venture, called The Perennial Seed Exchange. He hopes this service will grow into a healthy cousin to the more established Seed Savers Exchange in Iowa. That organization features vegetable seeds, whereas Skeeter's focus is on food-producing perennials, trees, and shrubs, especially those suited to the Northwest.

This dual emphasis on specific locale and perennials is not by chance. It reveals the direction of Skeeter's thinking and that of many in alternative agriculture. *Bioregion* and *permaculture* are the buzzwords. A central tenet of bioregionalism is that we should eat food grown in the region in which we live, hence the importance of discovering what food-producing plants could thrive locally and the importance of expanding the diversity of plants actually being grown. Bioregionalism is a decentralist notion: the essential boundaries are not artificial political ones; they are natural ones as defined by botany, geology, climate — plants, rivers and mountains, summer heat and winter cold.

Permaculture — Tasmanian Bill Molison's coinage for permanent agriculture — is self-sustaining food production, typically in a layout that incorporates fruits and nuts. In a sense, permaculture is to agriculture what edible landscaping is to gardening. Which is to say, there are no separate plots set aside for the growing of food, but rather the entire landscape is conceived so that it is simultaneously aesthetically pleasing and agriculturally productive. Furthermore, a permaculturally sound farm design would never require doses of exotic substances, any agricultural amendment derived from petroleum being exotic by definition. Thus the concept of permaculture, like that of organic farming, forbids the use of synthetic fertilizers and pesticides.

"Pick the right plant for the right place," Skeeter says, "and you can make just about any location productive. In this country, we try to convert the environment to suit the needs of the crop. You should choose the plants to suit the prevailing conditions — soil, climate — and you'll get productivity with less work. There are at least ten thousand or twenty thousand plants we could use for food. Everyone can eat like kings and queens, have the most varied, most nutritious diets the world has ever known, with locally grown foods."

"Water is magic here," says Muriel, Skeeter's partner.

Chelan is on the eastern slope of Washington's mountains. That is the dry side, where the average annual precipitation is a mere ten inches, even less in some places — not the drizzling West Coast, where envelopes glue themselves shut before you can slip the letter in. Most of that precipitation comes down as snow in winter, and on a fall day here at Muriel's, about twenty miles west of Chelan, the air is as dry as a technical report, with not even a wisp of a cloud in the blue sky.

Phyllis the goat has jumped up on the milking stand, and Muriel massages Bag Balm into the animal's teats prior to milking. Despite weeks without rain, about an acre of pasture for Phyllis and the six sheep is deep green. An automatic irrgation system dug by hand and fed by a mountain stream transforms this parched volcanic soil into lushness. In the large garden that provides Muriel with much of her income, fat boysenberries are ripening, and the late harvest of golden raspberries will follow after a couple more long days of bright sun and imported water.

Muriel is a broad, sturdy blond woman in sandals, T-shirt, and green cotton pants held with a drawstring and patched on both knees with corduroy. She milks with an easy familiar rhythm, as if on automatic pilot. Meanwhile Skeeter finishes bathing their week-old son, Ashley Conrad. Ashley is "dweller in the meadow by the ash tree," according to Skeeter. Muriel, who grew up in Switzerland, says that Conrad is a good Swiss name.

The family, which includes four-year-old Eli, Muriel's other son, gathers for breakfast at the summer kitchen, a roofed, open structure with running cold water and gas stove. Skeeter fries eggs from the chickens and fingerling potatoes from the garden. There is also a chewy homemade bread with Muriel's strawberry jam. Anise hyssop, picked from one of several herb plots near the kitchen, steeps in hot water, making a licorice-flavored tea. Colorado, the cat, is stalking a wild grouse that has been hanging around for days and seems to have a hankering for the domestic life. Sheppo, a sheepdoggish sort of creature, rests quietly nearby.

Muriel came to this steep patch of ground six years ago, and Skeeter joined her last year. Her husband had left, and she had broken her leg badly and needed help. Skeeter had met Muriel when he sold her some of the fruit trees planted at Whispering Pines, as she calls the mountainside homestead. She needed help, so he pitched in and has stayed on. This nuclear homestead is new to Skeeter, who in his late thirties still wears his graying hair in a ponytail. "So far, I've lived with groups, in intentional communities. Hundreds, even thousands of people, I consider my extended family. My old-age security is to have lots of friends. Friends will stand by you better in hard times than money."

Skeeter has reacted to his new domestic circumstances and responsibilities by increasing his annual income from about $2,000 to $3,000. He has also acquired a "new rig," a '77 Datsun station wagon. "It really cruises," Skeeter says proudly. "I can speed for the first time in years."

Friends of the Trees sometimes has enough funds so that Skeeter can pay himself a salary — all of $75 a month, pocket change by most late twentieth-century standards — and he usually hires out for several months to earn cash. As a kid in northern Michigan, he picked fruit, and he still does. "Now I'm at the top of the ladder. I'm one of the top hippie pickers," he says matter-of-factly, using the historical tag to describe himself. He can pick about a bin of apples an hour, worth $8 to $10 to him. Skeeter has also planted trees in the heavily logged Northwest, and he has picked wild huckleberries in season, making $140 a day in the mountains of Montana, where, he reports, "It was just us and the bears."

Muriel makes her living out of the garden, and after breakfast she starts trimming, weighing, and packing braids of garlic for market. She also has 200 pounds of shallots in the pantry, which will bring a couple of hundred dollars when sold. The shallots are next to the family's own stores: dried cherries, red-currant-and-cherry jam, crabapple-and-honey jam, lemon-peach butter, apricot "jus," and an arnica tincture. There are no pickles, however. Muriel explains: "I ran short last winter. I think it's true what they say of pregnant women and pickles."

Muriel is earthy, Skeeter more cerebral. His own description of himself is "bookworm." A class bully back in school pinned the nickname Skeeter on him: "I never knew what it meant. I was afraid that if I asked, he'd beat me up."

Since those early days, Skeeter has put conventional fears behind him. "It is better to be poor and happy than in the rat race — it is spiritually and psychologically damaging. If you have payments to make, then the idea of losing your job is frightening. I don't have to worry about big payments. I have the freedom of having nothing."

Skeeter's office is a shed, about eight feet by ten. Inside, on one wall are book-filled shelves of rough construction, and he maintains mailing lists for his various organizations and publications on cards in boxes. In addition to publishing a yearbook for the Friends of the Trees, he puts out the *Actinidia Enthusiast Newsletter*. For the moment, *actinidia* — hardy kiwi fruits — are the darlings of the gardening publications, which have been plumping for their virtues.

Skeeter knows that a computer would help him enormously with his work — a local orchardist lends him the use of his (appropriately named) Apple to typeset his publications — but having a computer in his office would allow Skeeter to accomplish quickly a number of tasks that he now does by hand, especially updating his mailing lists and expanding his index of plant species, which is a guide to plants and their various needs, including soil and water requirements, length of growing season, uses (food, forage, medicine), and such. Having a comprehensive index would

enable Skeeter to help people select from among the thousands of available perennial species and varieties those best
suited to a particular site. But a computer is a big-ticket item
for a man who has embraced voluntary simplicity and con-
siders a '77 Datsun a spiffy new rig.

Outside Skeeter's office is a garden — more a nursery —
of twenty by fifty feet, in which Skeeter is trying on various
plants for size. Specimens include

> European black currant;
> Chinese chestnut;
> American chestnut (concerted efforts
>   are underway to introduce this clas-
>   sic tree, once the dominant tree of
>   the eastern hardwood forests, into
>   areas of the Pacific Northwest that
>   do not harbor the blight responsible
>   for eliminating the handsome, ver-
>   satile species from the East);
> Hopi blue corn;
> millet;
> Siberian C peach rootstock, with the
>   graft high on the trunk to combat
>   winter injury;
> white mulberry, which is drought-
>   resistant;
> oak;
> buttercup squash;
> cantaloupe
> potatoes, which have more potassium
>   per ounce than bananas (take note,
>   endurance athletes and patients on

diuretics) and are not an exotic import like the banana;
hyssop, for herb tea, which could
eliminate our dependence on a couple of other exotic imports: coffee
and tea;
watermelon;
buffalo currant;
Nanking cherry, hardy and sweeter
than a pie cherry but tarter than a
sweet cherry;
autumn olive;
pecan ("I think we can grow pecans
here," Skeeter says, commenting
that in Chelan he came upon a
Dawn redwood, a tree usually
found only in milder areas);
Priscilla apples, with ants operating an
"aphid dairy" on the young trees:
the ants stroke the aphids to make
them produce a sweet "honeydew"
secretion, and at the same time the
ants protect the aphids from lady-
bugs. (To combat the aphids, which
damage the apple trees, Skeeter will
put a sticky substance called Tangle-
foot on the trunk of the tree to trap
the ants, leaving the aphids unprotected from predators.);
Siberian pea shrub, a bee food —
Skeeter is a cheerleader for bee
plants — a hedgerow plant, and

high-protein pea for game (and,
being leguminous, it fixes nitrogen
in the soil; in all, just the sort of
multipurpose plant that Skeeter is
promoting to those who will listen);
Russian olive, a nonleguminous
nitrogen-fixing tree;
and English and black walnuts. "Chelan has more walnuts per block
than any town I've ever been in,"
Skeeter says.

That's a quick tour through the experimental plot of a
man who says, "As a boy, I wanted to be a naturalist. That's
what I am now. All I have to do is get to central Asia." He
is drawn to that part of the world because climatic conditions there are similar to those in the northern United States,
and he believes he is likely to find many plants that are
promising in themselves or as material for breeding. Korea
proved a rich vein for the University of New Hampshire
plant breeder Elwyn Meader, whose celebrated introduc-
tions include the Reliance peach. Skeeter thinks unimagined
botanical riches must abound not only in Korea, but Mon-
golia, western Tibet, in Sinkiang Province in northwestern
China, and parts of the Soviet Union.

For now, though, Skeeter is tending to matters closer to
home. He and Eli are picking lunch from the garden while
Muriel nurses Ashley. Each time Eli spots a ripe tomato, he
exclaims, "Here's one!" Skeeter is almost as pleased with
the spearmint in bloom: "It's dancing with insects!"

Before the meal, Skeeter and Muriel offer a song of
thanksgiving:

Give thanks to the Mother Gaia,
Give thanks to the Father Sun,
Give thanks to the flowers in the garden
Where the Mother and Father are one.

As Skeeter says of his life of poverty: "I'm living high on the hog."

It is time to head into town. We're driving along the road that follows the south shore of Lake Chelan. This is an imposing lake, a glacial cut 55 miles long and 1,500 feet deep. Back in 1945, a school bus traveling along this road before it was widened went into the lake with fifteen children and a young driver. The bus and bodies were never recovered, the lake being so steep-sided and deep that divers never found the wreckage.

The lake empties into the Columbia River just to the east of town. The Columbia, which drains an area the size of France, literally powers the Pacific Northwest: eleven dams have been constructed in the U.S. along the Columbia's 1,214 miles, and with its tributaries it generates ten times as much electricity as the Colorado. The Columbia itself is also responsible for the Washington State apple industry, which produces half of the nation's crop.

You do not grow apples with twelve inches or less of precipitation annually. But you do grow apples if you have plentiful sunshine, fertile and well-drained soil, 150 or more days of good growing, and ample water. Chelan, Wenatchee, Cashmere, and south to Yakima have the sun, the soil, and the growing season. Ample water is not available from the sky, but it passes right by in the Columbia, so the orchardists simply pump it up into their orchards.

Come harvesttime, the hillsides hereabouts are toasted brown, dotted with the occasional ponderosa pine. There are a few patches of native bunchgrass, but mostly sage and bitterbrush have moved in. It's poor country, so poor, as the saying goes, that a jackrabbit would have to pack a lunch. But not where the irrigation flows. Color that the green of Eden.

In Washington State, 155,000 acres are planted to apples; 18,000 of those are Chelan County. (The county also has 9,000 acres of pears and cherries under cultivation.) All of the plantings are irrigated. Statewide, 68 to 70 million boxes of apples, 42 pounds to the box, will be harvested, the total value of the crop being $750 million. Considerable apple polishing.

When you think apple today, Red Delicious is likely to be the apple of your mind's eye, not perfectly round but longish and tapering, with five indentations at the blossom end. Most Washington apples are Red Delicious, because nowhere in the world can you grow them as well as you can in the eastern half of the state. The lack of humidity means russeting — speckling or roughening of the apple's skin — is rarely a problem. These fruits mature sleek and pretty. The sunny summer days promote growth, and the cool nights allow the trees to rest. Late in the season, when nighttime temperatures drop to the forties, the classic apple-red color develops. Around Chelan itself, for reasons no one fully understands, trees yield "typier" Red Delicious apples, those with the distinctive elongated shape.

There is some alarming chemistry in the apple-growing

business. Alar (daminozide) may have been dropped from the chemical arsenal, but that is the equivalent of the elimination of the B-1 bomber from the arms race. The State Cooperative Extension Service puts out a 92-page, 8½ by 11 *Spray Guide for Tree Fruits in Eastern Washington*, and there you can learn about the application of parathion, malathion, and guthion, to mention poisonous cousins for pest control, along with promalin and other hormonal cousins of Alar for thinning, color, and conformation. (In addition to the spraying done while the apples are growing, there is the whole pharmacology of postharvest treatment, which includes chemical baths and coating with fungicide and wax, for a spotless, lustrous finish.)

A "fraction of a fraction of a percent" of Washington's apples are grown organically — that is, without recourse to all this synthetic chemistry of uncertain safety. One orchardist who grows apples organically on thirteen of his thirty acres, a slender bearded man in his forties, son and grandson of orchardists, offered a tour of his place. He asked not to be identified by name; he does not want trouble from his apple-growing neighbors, all of whom spray with synthetic chemicals. "The thing you have to understand," he says, "is that a lot of my neighbors don't understand what I'm trying to do. I have to live in the apple-growing community."

Mr. Greenleaf, I'll call him, was having trouble with coddling moth, a common orchard pest. A coddling moth "hit" mars the apple's surface, and if the larva actually penetrates the skin and worms its way into the apple, the fruit is a total loss. Greenleaf has sprayed against coddling moth with ryania, a botanical poison derived from a Caribbean plant, and his crew has been culling damaged apples, which he estimates make up approximately 3 percent of the crop. "Some neighbors would be appalled," Greenleaf says in reference to the damage to the developing crop. "They would say, 'My God, I'm going to report you.' " Being reported for failure to control a major pest would mean that the county pest-control agency could require Greenleaf to spray his orchard — and not with ryania — to combat the problem. "When I first had a coddling-moth problem," Greenleaf recounts, "a bunch of growers got up a petition, but my neighbors, whom I've been in good contact with, wouldn't sign it."

Some in the apple-growing community hold the view that the few organic orchardists in the region get by without using synthetic chemicals only because their orchards are hidden among those that are sprayed. That is, the organic orchardists obtain their pest control by riding piggyback on the spraying schedules of conventional growers. Such a view fails, however, to take into account what organic agriculture means at its core.

At the most basic level, organic practitioners simply avoid using synthetic "inputs": that is, fertilizer and pesticides. Instead of spraying a synthetically formulated toxin to control coddling moth, an organic practitioner might spray the botanically based ryania. In a crucial way, though, organic agriculture is much more than the mere substitution of a biological input — manure, say — for a chemical input: anhydrous ammonia. Organic agriculture seeks to build on an understanding of the fundamental ecology of a farm and to make the various interrelationships work together and sustain each other. Hence, other approximate terms for organic agriculture include "ecological" agriculture and "sustainable" agriculture.

One of the basic practices of organic agriculture is crop

rotation. Rotating helps to build a fertile soil, in good tilth; it combats pests — the populations of specific insects will increase dangerously only if their preferred food is provided in large uninterrupted blocks year after year. A crop rotation is only a part of organic agriculture as a whole, but it is also an analog of organic agriculture, because a rotation is based on a diversity of crops, and in such variety there is strength and stability. Ideally, the organic farm includes livestock, and their manure feeds the soil (which is rich in a diversity of organisms), which in turn grows the feed.

At its deepest level, organic farming is a way to return the power in agriculture to the farmer. Conventional, or chemical, farmers depend on a host of off-farm resources — experts and their technological by-products. Organic farmers, in contrast, rely on their own knowledge of the way in which the natural world and their own farms work.

Organic agriculture in its purest form is small-scale, diversified, and labor-intensive. It can be practiced on a large scale in less than ideal fashion, and it can be monocultural — only apples, say — but inevitably, it requires skilled hands, like the agriculture of old. Greenleaf employs eight or nine full-time workers, twice as many as is the current standard for an orchard his size. "He spends money on people rather than chemicals" is Skeeter's analysis.

"Herbicides are cheaper," Greenleaf's wife says. "But we can sell our apples for a couple dollars more a box because they're organic," Greenleaf notes.

The higher price that organic produce commands has provided a target for critics, who say that costly organic food is the food of the elite. But organic food is safe food, for both the consumer and the environment, and comes without hidden costs that the taxpayers will bear for environmentally insensitive farming: the incredible cost of cleaning up groundwater pollution throughout major agricultural areas, the medical costs to farmers especially, but consumers as well, for cancers and other health problems associated with chemically rich agriculture, the social costs of the disruption of our agricultural communities resulting from large-scale agriculture made possible by chemicals. So the consumer may indeed pay more for an organic apple at the cash register, but, in the long run, that apple is a good — and economical — buy.

There is the story, perhaps apocryphal, of the man from Oregon who arrived in Chelan at harvest season and loaded his truck with cull apples from one of the local warehouses. He boasted that he was taking the small, misshapen, and blemished fruit home to sell at a premium as organic. Greenleaf admits, "We've got to be able to market blemishes — that is the key." But the fruits remaining on Greenleaf's trees are handsome, proving that an organic apple need not be fruit's equivalent of the Hunchback of Notre Dame.

Orchard work, by its nature, requires a lot of labor. Picking requires the most, then in descending order come thinning, pruning, propping (using stakes to support bearing limbs that otherwise might break under the weight of their fruit.) Increasingly orchardists are planting to save labor; they do that by using dwarfing rootstock. Dwarf trees are easier to prune, easier to pick. The trees are trained to a central leader, instead of having an open center, and this shape eliminates the need for propping. Dwarfing stock also starts bearing sooner and can be planted at greater densities. Typically today, orchards are being planted at 350 to 650 trees per acre, up from 250 trees per acre ten years ago. But the longevity of these orchards declines; an orchard planted today might last twenty years, fifteen if planted at the highest densities, but ten years ago, orchards had a twenty-five-year life span.

In some respects, Chelan is just a section at the north end of the great Washington apple factory, which, like an egg factory or a milk factory or any other agricultural factory, is refining its techniques and pushing its units for higher production. Work the trees/cows/chickens hard. Use them up. Throw them out.

"The Columbia River orchards are a monoculture. They are deficient ecologically," says Phil Unterscheutz, who supplies Greenleaf and other organic growers with fertilizers and materials for pest management. "Nobody can grow a pristine apple in this valley. We're living in a real toxic environment."

We're on the top of Chelan Butte, elevation 3,892 feet, the launching pad for the national hang-gliding championships. Skeeter has picked a sprig of sagebrush. "Here's something to take home," he says. "The Indians considered it a sacred herb, an herb to dispel bad spirits." Skeeter starts chanting.

Spending time with Skeeter reminds one of the perils to the planet in the late twentieth century: the erosion of the soil, the combustion of fossil fuels tainting the air, the decimation of the earth's forests, the toxicity of our agriculture, and the general wastefulness of our ways.

"It looks pretty dismal to me when I think about the United States and how we're going to get from where we are to something sustainable. We're depleting the world. We're the vampire. The extravagant life style has got to crash.

"When you look at the world situation, it's pretty grim. But when you look at it cosmically, there's nothing to worry about. I'm willing to see this civilization crumble. I would rather heal the earth than prop up this civilization.

"A lot of people think it's foolish to work for a better world. They think: if you don't tread on anyone, that's about as good as you can do. But one person can make a difference. A lot of people have given up on that idea."

So Skeeter, who has for years been expecting the apocalypse, first the revolution and now the sunset of this civilization, remains utopian. "You bet! I'm a social visionary. I've always been doing something that wouldn't make money, following some dream. The world needs out-and-out radicals to show people where the middle of the road is."

And, according to Skeeter, everywhere along the road, people should be planting trees: "It is better to give a tree to an enemy who will care for it than to a friend who will let it die.

"I think trees are one of the most political things in the world. The political vanguard won't do a bit of good if the world's ecosystem is collapsing around us." Ultimately, Skeeter can view even that catastrophe with equanimity: "I'm an eternal being," he says. "This life is just one step on the path."

No one can say with certainty just where this mortal path leads, but while he is following it, Skeeter — full-bearded, hair graying, poor, happy, and hopeful — is networking hard on behalf of those who would live the good life and the right life in the Pacific Northwest.

And afterward? "I may be transferred out of the solar system."

Chapter 5

THE FLICKERVILLE MOUNTAIN DUET

DOTT, PENNSYLVANIA — At Johnnie's Motel & Diner, which is as good as they come in Fulton County, a room costs $19 a night, plus tax. For that price, you don't get color TV, but the set is hooked up to the cable. Breakfast at the diner, a short walk across the blacktop parking lot, costs $2.97, including tip, for two eggs (any style), toast, hash browns, and coffee. The "butter" is a soybean product, even though this is dairy country.

Johnnie's is in McConnellsburg, the county seat, on the eastern edge of Fulton County. Situated at the foot of Tuscarora Mountain, which effectively protects the county from more populous and developed parts of Pennsylvania to the east, McConnellsburg looks out on Big Cove, a lovely broad valley of rich soil given over to dairy farms. To get to Dott, you have to travel some fifteen miles to the southwest, which is the way the Appalachian Mountains run here (past the last campsite in Pennsylvania of Confederates retreating from Gettysburg), over several ridges, through several valleys and back up onto Tonoloway Ridge.

Once in Dott, you will find a grocery store and seventeen

houses. Until 1982 there were 30,000 laying hens as well. Outside the store, two old-timers are comparing double-hernia operations, complaining about hospital costs, and, from time to time, cupping their hands and holding them near their crotches, as if to reinforce the work of their surgeons.

Inside the store, it is dark. All the lights are off except the one over the counter on which sits a mechanical adding machine and cash register. Although physically large, the store offers a limited range of groceries and a few garden tools. Danny Lanehart, the proprietor, in his early thirties, wears glasses and green work shirt and pants. He says that he used to carry some hardware, but it didn't move.

An elderly woman comes in to tell Danny about a young man who died in the hospital of injuries suffered about a month earlier at the family's sawmill. The deceased, a three-hundred-pounder, fell through some planks onto the mill's drive shaft, which simply kept spinning, stripping off his clothes and snapping his bones.

When Lanehart introduces the messenger to me, she launches into a tale of alcohol and domestic mayhem, of cars running off the road and of doors and furniture being burned for heat in the wood stove. The narrative takes turns like the roads hereabouts, and insofar I can follow, I gather that on occasion it involves her son, a man of indeterminate age who stands nearby in baggy coveralls, holding a gallon tub of ice cream and grinning whenever his name is mentioned.

The area around Dott is home to a good number of small sawmills and rough folk. The county is a poor one. It has neither a bookstore nor a movie theater. When I returned

home to Vermont and found my car sandwiched between a
Saab Turbo and a Volvo in the airport parking lot, I realized
I had not seen a pricey foreign car for a week, not that I
missed such vehicles. The women in Fulton County still
wear slacks, not the sweat pants that so widely have become
the garment of choice in other places, where the fashions —
or simply the times — spin wildly, like the cherries in the
window of a slot machine.

"The people in Fulton County don't want Fulton County
to change very much," Danny Lanehart says, echoing what
Don Palmer, the county agent, told me: "When I came
here twelve years ago, people said, 'Help us stay the way
we are.' "

"The people in Fulton County are very conservative,"
Danny Lanehart says. "The last Democrat Fulton County
went for was FDR."

On the edge of town, in the cemetery beside the white
United Church of Christ building, a song sparrow sings from
the top of a gravestone of one of the many Mellotts buried
here. A good many more Mellotts (sometimes Melott) are
still alive all over the county. One owns the New Holland/
Ford tractor dealership in McConnellsburg.

Another runs the Saturday-night auction. Bearded, with
a gravelly voice, he tries to drum up interest in a used
shovel, a quilt, bunches of bananas, carrots bagged in some
faraway state — "pulled out of the ground this morning,"
he says, peddling his vegetables with a pitch that is the produce vendor's equivalent of the used-car salesman's "only-
one-owner-a-little-old-lady-who-just-drove-it-to-church-
on-Sunday." The auctioneer's wife, a stylish blond smoking
a slim, filtered cigar and wearing a bright red sweater, gives

him a disgusted look. The auction barn smells of french fries. The crowd thins out. The auctioneer offers coins to bidders: two buffalo nickels, then a dime dated 1895, and finally three steel pennies from 1943. A fifty-cent bid takes the pennies. He is now down to the dregs: an old record player without a speaker: "Who will give me five dollars?" Short pause. "One dollar?" Shorter pause. "Fifty cents?" Almost no pause. "A quarter?" He adds another record player to the lot, and one bidder apparently figures, "What the hell," and offers a quarter to buy them both. As the auction draws to a close, another quarter buys you an old blanket and a lampshade, offered together to make the lot more appealing. Or you might simply decide the time has come to head home for the night.

Cecil Mellott runs the Mellott Wood Preserving Company — "the creosote plant," as it is known locally — just outside of Needmore, a few miles north of Dott. He started the operation ten years ago and says 99 percent of this business is treating railroad ties for Conrail, which buys about 200,000 of them a year from him. Mellott says he grew up cutting railroad ties. The wood, preferably red oak, which absorbs the preservative better than other hardwoods, comes from a hundred-mile radius. That keeps expanding, largely because of the gypsy moths, which have been feasting on the hardwood hillsides around here since 1982. Mellott buys many of the timbers he treats from his brothers; one runs a sawmill across the road, and another has a sawmill a quarter of a mile down the hill.

Mellott has a beard that is turning gray, and, taking no chances, he wears both camouflage suspenders and a belt to keep his pants up. His assessment of his home ground:

"Everybody says Fulton County's a good place to come to sleep."

Far from being a weekend to sleep in, it will be a busy time at Flickerville Mountain Farm and Groundhog Ranch, located some two miles to the west of Dott. The list of chores noted on lined yellow paper includes twenty-four items, written in capital letters in a firm, clear hand. SAWDUST ON BERRIES. LAY DRIP LINES. TILL CORN PATCH. CHARGE SPRAYER. CHARGE BATTERY. FINISH PEA STAKES, and so on. Eight more items have been jotted down by a second, less bold hand: spray stone fruit, finish/hang red traps, Foliagro peas, spray coles with Hinder. In addition, the list calls for the planting of fourteen kinds of herbs, vegetables, and flowers, and the harvesting of asparagus and spinach. It is never a leisure retreat to the country for the *Washington Post* reporters Cass Peterson and Ward Sinclair when, every weekend during the growing season, they make the hundred-ten-mile drive from suburban Virginia to Flickerville Mountain Farm, where they have an organic market garden, with six acres under cultivation.

Although Peterson and Sinclair surely live divided lives, interviewing cabinet officers during the week and doing stoop labor on weekends, there is also a connection between their vocation as Washington journalists and their avocation as dirt farmers in the Appalachian hills.

Peterson, who is in her late thirties, seems tentative, perhaps wary, and is easy to underestimate — before joining the *Post* eight years ago, she won a settlement in a sex-discrimination suit when some editors at another newspaper took her lightly. In recent years she has covered first the

Environmental Protection Agency and now the Interior and Energy departments — the "Gloom-and-Doom beat." As a journalist, Peterson has gained theoretical familiarity with pesticides, fungicides, water policy, and such. As a farmer, she makes hands-on, everyday decisions about those things.

Sinclair is a rumpled skeptic in his early fifties. "Our most elusive reporter," a colleague at the *Post* calls him. He wears glasses, has bags under his eyes, and undisciplined graying curls. He earned both undergraduate and graduate degrees from the University of Mexico, where he studied after getting out of the service, even though he spoke no Spanish when he pulled into Mexico City the summer before he enrolled.

He has covered Congress for the *Post* ("Greed-and-Lust beat") and was assigned to Agriculture in 1981 at the time of Jimmy Carter's grain embargo. At first, he felt that he had been exiled to reportorial Siberia. "I thought I was being punished. It took me about two weeks to realize I had been handed a gold mine. Agriculture is easily the most interesting thing I've been assigned to cover. It has allowed me to travel and forced me to meet people I otherwise wouldn't have. Most of my agricultural-reporting career has been spent covering farmers who aren't making it, but it's given me an appreciation for our country: I've met people who have survived and come out stronger, overcoming adversity."

At the same time, Sinclair adds, "I've talked to farmers who would never make it because they had no imagination, no flexibility — they wouldn't diversify. I would like to try to be an example."

Chance as much as conviction led Peterson and Sinclair to the farm. One of their colleagues at the *Post* had bought a place nearby, put in a tennis court, and when he and his family drove up on weekends, they enjoyed the good life, not the peasant life. Once, when visiting, Peterson and Sinclair told their host that he ought to think about doing something with the land, at least put in a garden. His response was to tell them, several weeks later, that a nearby farm had come up for sale, and if they were so keen on tilling the soil, here was their chance.

Almost on a whim they made a bid. It was not accepted, but shortly thereafter, they heard about another place that would be offered at auction. When the gavel came down, they were the inexperienced owners of sixty-five acres, fifty tillable; a house with asphalt-shingle siding, a leaky roof, starlings nesting in the attic, and wiring that, according to the electrician, seemed rigged to burn the place down; three sturdy outbuildings, and several less so, including a hundred-foot-long, guano-encrusted chicken house.

In the summer of 1983 they started gardening, and, finding themselves with a surplus, they began to think about selling it. Thus a second career was born.

A number of considerations led them to grow organically, Peterson says. "I've gardened with every conceivable chemical; now, given my experience as a reporter, my concern is not just human health. I've also become concerned with the environment."

Sinclair cites what he calls "two signal events" in his decision to adhere to organic practices. The first occurred when he mixed diazinon — a pesticide — in a plastic cup, which then disintegrated. "The house smelled like a chemical factory," he recalls. (Diazinon, a widely used chemical included in many home-and-garden pesticide formulations, has been implicated in numerous instances of wildlife deaths, even in cases when it has been applied according to the manufacturer's recommendations.)

The second took place when, by chance, he happened to study the label of a bottle of captan, a potent fungicide. By all appearances, it was an innocuous compound, but Sinclair noticed a dotted line on the label, which he proceeded to cut. The label folded out, and there, hidden from the unsuspecting consumer, were all the warnings — dire ones indeed. (As a group, fungicides are among the agricultural chemicals most threatening to human health, and the Environmental Protection Agency recently has issued rulings reducing their — and captan's — allowable uses.)

In an important way, even though Peterson and Sinclair have come to farming relatively late in their lives, they are fortunate. As Peterson says, "We had to start from scratch and learn how to do this. We didn't have any large-scale chemical habits to unlearn."

Sinclair continues the train of thought: "Two generations of farmers have come of age in chemical agriculture, and I think the first victim of these chemicals is the farmer himself. If drinking water becomes contaminated, the first well to go bad is the farmer's.

"These chemicals are hanging heavy in the minds of many farmers I have spoken with. I understand the trepidation they feel about declining yields if they make the transition from chemicals. And I sympathize with their inability to get good information on the subject. But those farmers who are doing agriculture like their grandfathers — except they have John Deere tractors and sophisticated implements — those people are invariably successful economically."

As Sinclair speaks, he is putting up pea fence in one of

the fifteen 120-foot rows of peas that he and Peterson have planted. Above the pea beds are 200 young fruit trees — apple, peach, and pear — and the long-range plan is to extend the orchard down the slope, but at a cost of about $8 per tree, expansion will have to be gradual.

When I spoke with them, Peterson and Sinclair had sunk between $90,000 and $100,000 into their farming venture. The farm itself cost them $70,000; machinery ran between $15,000 and $20,000. They started with the favored implement of home gardeners all over, a Troy-Bilt rototiller, but after wearing out a set of tines in a single season, they graduated to real farm equipment. Their first tractor was a high-clearance Farmall A, a traditional row-crop tractor, and more recently they have acquired a new compact tractor, a four-wheel-drive Ford 1310, with a fifty-two-inch rotary tiller. For implements they have a plastic-mulch layer and a "Docovator." The mulch layer is a simple device that will lay down 100 feet of black plastic in a couple of minutes, far more quickly than can be done by hand; it also puts down the soil-warming, weed-suppressing plastic in a taut, straight row. The "Docovator" is an inexpensive one-of-a-kind device that turns tilled strips of soil into raised beds for planting. It was customer-fabricated by a nearby equipment dealer, the eponymous Doc Hoover. Pulled behind the tractor, the Docovator has large double disks set the width of the tilled bed; these are toed out, so they mound the soil into the middle of the bed. A steel frame welded behind the disks then smooths and levels the top of the mounded soil, creating a bed ready for planting.

Peterson and Sinclair have spent another several thousand dollars on fruit and berry stock, fertilizer, stakes, chicken wire, sprayer, and assorted tools. One of those is the stapler Sinclair is using to tack up pea fence, except when distracted by my conversation, he shoots a staple in his finger. Cursing and grimacing, he extracts it and sucks on the twin dots of blood that appear like a snakebite.

Mistakes are not uncommon: Peterson and Sinclair have discovered that raising acres of crops for market is decidedly different from raising vegetables in a home garden. "You really notice what vegetables germinate well," Peterson says. Sugar Daddy snap peas have not, for example, and the germination of monogerm beets has not been promising. Most beet seeds actually have several seeds inside the husk. This attribute makes for good germination, but means that painstaking thinning is necessary. The monogerm seed — one seed per husk — would eliminate the demands of thinning, but with such poor germination, the solution has proven as troublesome as the original problem.

Other difficulties the pair faces result from their peculiar part-time, long-distance status. "We're overextended," Peterson says. "We lose crops just because we don't have the time we need to do everything." One weekend early this year, as daylight faded on a Sunday evening, they gambled on the weather and decided not to cover their peppers and cherry tomatoes. They lost the gamble to a late frost.

Despite such setbacks, Peterson and Sinclair's diligence has not gone unnoticed by their neighbors in Fulton County, although few know them by name. The market garden, row after tilled row separated by strips of sod, is an eye-catching sight, and these strangers who arrive and push themselves all weekend are the source of some speculation. Besides which, they have that new Ford tractor, which is viewed locally as a sure sign of prosperity.

Sinclair recounts an exchange he had one evening at the

auction barn. A man with whom he had a nodding acquaintance sidled up and remarked: "They say you're doing real well at that place of yours."

"We're doing OK," Sinclair responded, suspecting the fellow was more interested in eliciting information than in offering compliments.

"They say you're doing real well," the fellow repeated, apparently determined to find out what he was after, but equally determined to keep his inquiry indirect.

"It's going OK," Sinclair said again, keeping his interrogator at bay. He chuckles at this point. "The guy just couldn't bring himself to ask us what we were up to, but he figured we wouldn't be working so hard for the plain fun of it, and since we were driving a new tractor, we must be making a killing.

"Actually," he says, "we're losing our asses."

That's not true, actually, as Sinclair then admits. Flickerville Mountain Farm and Groundhog Ranch is not yet profitable, but it grossed $1,100 in 1984 and income more than doubled every year after for the next three years. Peterson and Sinclair have continued to see an upward revenue trend. To accomplish that, they do not take summer vacations. During the marketing season, they take every Friday off from work and head to the farm. They harvest Friday afternoon and evening, sometimes aided by flashlight, and then get up at 4:30 on Saturday mornings, so they can be set up at the Hagerstown, Maryland, farmers' market by six o'clock. They also harvest Sunday afternoons to fill orders from a couple of dozen colleagues at the *Post*. In addition, they have contracts for Sugar Snap peas, cherry tomatoes, purple cauliflower, bok choy, and Chinese cabbage to fill with a Maryland-based wholesale distributor of organic produce, and they deliver to him Sunday nights before resuming their lives as journalists. Sinclair comments that he no longer reads novels or general nonfiction, but rather, all his reading time is devoted to horticultural and agricultural literature.

The pair has learned some tricks along the way. They do not grow sweet corn, which fetches eight cents an ear. They do grow decorative Indian corn, for which they can command forty cents an ear. They have found that the flower statice is a terrific cash crop for part-time growers: it resists frost and drought and pests; it can be sold fresh, and it also dries extremely well. When selling herbs, they discovered that instead of selling them individually, it is more profitable to make up "kits for spaghetti sauce," which include a recipe and all the necessary fresh ingredients: basil, oregano, plum tomatoes, peppers, and onions.

They have had to find crops that fit their schedule, unlike green beans. "It took all day to pick eight cases," Sinclair says, "and we get twelve dollars a case." This recollection prompts Sinclair to remark, "We've had some hot arguments about pricing," with Sinclair inclined to price more aggressively.

The Flickerville Mountain Duet have agreed that they cannot do all the grunt labor alone. To get inexpensive help, they speculate about the possibility of taking on apprentices — temporary serfs, in effect — something that a number of organic growers around the country have done. Instead they have hired a diligent high-school student, Jared Linscott, to work alongside them during weekends.

Sinclair calls the summer routine "grueling." Peterson admits that it is "schizophrenic at times." When an appealing beat at the *Post* opened up, she had to concede that she could not be seriously considered if she was determined to leave town every Friday. But she adds, "One of the things we get from this place is fun."

"Farmers are living one of the best-kept secrets in the country," Sinclair says. "The freedom, the excitement — seeing a pea cracking through the soil — it's spiritual."

As Sinclair speaks, I can feel myself resonating to his words — give up the computer keyboard and the printer's galleys and all those little words, facile words, hollow words, and take up the tractor's controls, the spading fork, the hoe, the package of seeds — small bundles of the life force. Enough of desks and deadlines and corporate intrigue. How uplifting it would be to walk outside into the country air and feel the sunlight (or rain, for that matter) streaming down and the moist rich soil underfoot, and to bend my back to the task of aiding things grow. Perhaps such lyrics have limited appeal. There was a time years ago when it was a siren song to many — "back to the land" was the mantra. Well, I am in the country and on the land, but I still live the secondhand life, the journalist's life. And that may be why Sinclair's experience and his words are so powerful to me, a writer/editor always one step removed from the action.

Unlike me, Sinclair and Peterson eventually took the bold step, put down their tape recorders for good. After almost five years of leading a dual existence, they gave up watching the action. They sank a deep well for irrigation, reducing the risks a dry year would bring, and they have become full-time farmers now. They are loving the change, and I envy them the immediacy of their days, the physical tiredness, the small satisfactions that make life worth living.

These two veteran reporters have come down from the observation tower, giving up the safety available to a clever person who would dare no more than a critique. No longer reporting the dirt, they are happily mucking about in it. And rightly proud of the decision they have made.

They have put a lot of miles and figurative distance as well between themselves and Washington, D.C. They have become Dott, a modest, proud little place, where chickens once scratched in the dirt and dairy cows still graze, where the land, if treated right, still offers a decent living.

"I can't tell you the thrill it is to walk through the parking lot during a break at the market when someone recognizes me as a vendor. They nod with an incredible kind of deference," Sinclair says. "I don't want to overstate it, but they're saying: 'This person grows food.' "

Chapter 6

THE ROMANCE OF THE GRAPE

KEUKA LAKE, NEW YORK — Peter Johnstone's cellar is damp, cool, and yeasty. Big stainless-steel tanks run along the cinder-block walls. White hoses and black extension cords trail across the puddled, concrete floor. A movable pump sits at one end of the cellar; Johnstone moves it to the other end.

He is preparing to transfer fluid from one tank to another, and he hooks up the hose. He climbs a ladder to the top of one tank and opens a valve. Then, with flashlight and measuring stick in hand, he climbs up to the top of another tank. He starts the pump and peers down the beam of the flashlight into the splashing darkness. After several minutes, the fluid reaches the desired level, and Johnstone shuts off the pump.

"My job is mainly moving liquids around," he says. So much for the romance of being a winemaker.

Johnstone is a small, trim man with tousled gray hair. His face is ruddy, impish, and he is wearing shorts, T-shirt, and running shoes with dark socks. Having finished his morning jog, Johnstone is back at his work in the basement of Heron Hills Winery, which he and a partner own.

In 1968, he came from a New York City advertising

agency to the western shore of Keuka Lake between Hammondsport and Branchport, where he took over an ordinary Finger Lakes region vineyard. He set about transforming its twenty-five acres of native grapes by planting French *vinifera* varieties, the source of fine wines. Nine years after his arrival, Johnstone started a small winery, and, in certain important respects, his journey is representative of what is happening in the lake country of the state that is, after California, the nation's largest producer of grapes and wines.

New York wines have never been known as good wines. Typically, they have been sweet and grapey and heavy — like spiked Welch's grape juice. Here, in what is one of the world's coldest wine-making regions, winemakers have relied not on the best wine grapes — the *vinifera* varieties — but on the grapes that grew best, the native *labrusca* varieties: Catawbas, Concords, Delawares, and Niagaras. In small but significant ways, that situation is in ferment.

Someday, Peter Johnstone thinks, the Finger Lakes region will be known as the source of America's premier white wines. Located in north-central New York, the region's lakes run in vertical strips from Syracuse on the east to Rochester on the west. Keuka Lake is the third largest of the eleven lakes, after Geneva and Seneca lakes. Having been chiseled by glaciers, the Finger Lakes are narrow and deep: Keuka is 187 feet deep, neighboring Seneca, 632 feet. Of the wines produced along the shores of these waters, Johnstone says, "Our whites are not flabby the way California's are."

A flabby wine? One that is low in acid, a condition that results from the greater heat and extended final ripening that occur in California. Johnstone says cool falls make New York whites — Chardonnay and Riesling, especially — acid and crisp. But the upstate New York cold can be a problem too, preventing full ripening. Then the grapes lack sufficient sugar.

Johnstone knows about the cold, having acquired a vineyard that can on a winter morning register temperatures that are ten degrees lower than those at neighboring fields. Knowing what he does now, he admits that he might have an easier time of it if he grew his grapes on nearby Seneca Lake to the east. Being larger and deeper, Seneca Lake has not frozen since 1902, so its water effectively moderates winter temperatures. Nonetheless, Johnstone's delicate *vinifera* grapevines have survived and his Rieslings have done particularly well.

In a promotional flier, Johnstone describes his Johannisberg Riesling: "Estate Bottled, 100% of the varietal named. Near dry with that intense flowery bouquet characteristic of Mosel Rieslings. Hint of apricot at the finish. Great first-course choice."

A translation of the flier reveals that the winery is also the vineyard that actually grew the grapes that provided the juice for the wine, which is made entirely of the Riesling variety. The dryness refers to sweetness or lack thereof; in this case, fermentation has almost eliminated the sugar, all but 1 percent. The juice would have started at about 19 percent sugar. As for the bouquets and apricots, that's vintner's jargon for what one social commentator has called hee-haw and bullshit.

(If, however, Johnstone's description of his Riesling strikes you as a touch florid, compare it to another local winery's prose about its Riesling: "Semi-dry, earthy nose with hints of apricot. Complex mouth finishes crisp with a touch of sweetness." Men have circled the globe in search of such a woman.)

Johnstone's Johannisberg Riesling, whatever the charac-
terization, is no slouch: the wine has won a gold medal
in eight consecutive vintages, the only wine ever to have
done so. Or so Johnstone asserts: "The way we found out,"
he says, "is that we made the claim and nobody com-
plained." Heron Hill's 1984 Riesling was, Johnstone says,
"the first New York wine in thirty-five years to win a gold
medal in California."

As a one-time adman, Johnstone is well aware of the
importance of image in the wine game, and he is obviously
proud of his record and pleased to have the recognition that
awards bring. Yet he reveals an intelligent skepticism about
the significance of awards: "This reverence for medals — it's
promotion, sales. There's a lot of luck in winning," Johnstone says. "You have to make a technically good wine, but
out of the sixty-five Rieslings at San Diego [where his 1984
vintage won], you know there had to be some good ones.
So what makes ours a gold-medal winner?"

Apparently the luck of the draw, as well as the merits of
the wine. "You don't want to follow a sweet wine, because
yours would taste tart in comparison," Johnstone explains.
"And you want to be at the front of the tasting, because the
judges will have fatiguing palates."

Heron Hill is a "farm winery," one of 54 in New York
state. The definition of farm winery is one that may produce
a maximum of 50,000 gallons of wine a year, allowing it to
operate under somewhat relaxed regulations. Heron Hill annually produces 33,000 gallons, which yield Johnstone "a
good living." And enough profit so that he is expanding.

Statewide, 81 wineries produce 30 million gallons of
wine each year, so Johnstone's production barely exceeds
one-tenth of 1 percent of New York's total. Still, his output

is significant because he is a leader in the transition to the fine wines that win over the tastemakers.

Art Hunt does not have Peter Johnstone's style, but someday his wines might compete with Johnstone's. That is what he is hoping for.

The Hunts backed into winemaking. Art Hunt and his wife, Joyce, moved from Corning, New York, to take over the family vineyard up the hills from the blinking light in the center of what passes for Branchport. For eight years, the Hunts simply grew grapes on the fertile, well-drained glacial soil that slopes down to Keuka Lake. They had eighteen acres of native Concords when they started and have increased their plantings to seventy-five acres of several varieties. Having success growing grapes does not, however, necessarily result in success selling them — not just for the Hunts, but for grape growers throughout the region.

Grape supply outstripped grape and juice demand. Who drinks grape juice for breakfast? There are bigger problems as well, as James Tresize of the New York Wine/Grape Foundation explains: "Probably more damaging was the international situation. We didn't overplant in New York — vineyard acreage has been shrinking for ten years. There were vast subsidized European plantings. There was a wine lake in Europe, more like a wine ocean — millions of gallons were unsold. With a strong dollar, the effect was to make European wines so inexpensive that it was impossible for American wine producers to compete." In addition, U.S. per capita wine consumption flattened out in 1982 and then dropped off in 1985.

With the glut, growers are getting as little as half as much as they were ten years ago for grapes that now cost three times as much to grow. The great popularity of wine coolers has been only a partial salvation — the coolers are, like a sponge, sopping up much of the surplus grape juice as Americans thirstily sop up the coolers, but the price paid for grapes that go into coolers remains well below production costs.

Having seen their annual income from growing grapes decline from $140,000 to an unprofitable $75,000, the Hunts decided that they could not just sit and wait for the market to rebound. Instead, they would do as a number of small-scale farmers have done: they would transform their basic crop into a specialty product — add value, that is — and sell the resulting processed goods at a higher price. The gamble is simple: that the premium that buyers pay for the specialty item — wine, in this case — is greater than the additional cost of making it. "We were producing the finest grapes anyone could grow," Art Hunt says, "but no one wanted them. With a winery, we have control over our future because we can retail our farm product ourselves."

The Hunts made their first batch of wine — 2,000 gallons — in 1981. In 1985, with new equipment, they made 18,500 gallons; annual production of 30,000 gallons is in sight. And beyond that?

Without hesitation, Art says, "We hope to be the premium winery of moderate size in the East."

Define "moderate." Art: "Two hundred fifty thousand gallons." And Joyce immediately interjects, uneasily, at Art's direct, bold, and unprotected response: "Jeeze, Art, don't . . ." but her voice trails off.

A small winery capable of producing 30,000 gallons can cost several hundred thousand dollars to set up. In their first years of making wine, the Hunts improvised and shopped for bargains, but with more ambitious plans, they needed money. So they found investors and incorporated Finger Lakes Wine Cellars as a separate entity from Hunt Farms, which grows the grapes. "Originally wine-making was a marketing device," Art says. "Then it took on a life of its own."

One consequence of the winery's new life is that the Hunts had to give up some control to the investors and board of directors (whom cautious Joyce declines to name). But Art seems undaunted by the demands of business partners. "We still have voting control," he says. "It is better to have a shared interest in a going concern than full interest in one that's going under. If you want to get rich, make a fortune elsewhere — and then lose it in the wine business. My goal is to make a living."

To do that, the Hunts have a multifaceted plan: They are polishing the image of Finger Lakes Wine Cellars. They have changed the logo on their bottles to a stylish design featuring the F and L of Finger Lakes, having abandoned a folksy logo that pictures a farmhouse. (The "Wine Cellar" at F/L is actually a converted dairy barn.)

Also, Finger Lakes Wine Cellars is buying fancy *vinifera* grapes for as much as $1,000 a ton, so it can make first-rate Chardonnay and Riesling wines. Art describes his vineyard as "one of the best overall sites for growing grapes," but he acknowledges that the *vinifera* varieties do better elsewhere, so he buys them. "The best wines are made from the best grapes — that's axiomatic," Art says.

In addition, with the help of a U.S. Department of Agriculture grant, the Hunts are trying an experimental grafting program, unique in the East, to transform their seventy-five acres of vines from native varieties to French-American hybrids, like Seyval and Ravat (or Vignoles). "We'll probably never plant another native grape," Hunt says. Although the drinking public is unfamiliar with these French-American hybrids, they make better wines than native grapes, yet are less finicky to grow than *vinifera* grapes. (One young woman who works at the winery said with a knowing glint that the Finger Lakes "late harvest" Ravat, which is made from grapes paradoxically blessed by a fungus, is an "aphrodisiac.")

Hunt Farms still sells its grapes to other commercial wineries and offers grape juice to home winemakers. Art even makes noises about growing table grapes, at which suggestion Joyce starts to wear her worried face. Once the vineyards are producing only the more desirable varieties, Hunt Farms will sell primarily to Finger Lakes Wine Cellars, and the Hunts will have created a ready and profitable market for their grapes. They will also have a piece of the potentially lucrative action on the wine sales.

Finger Lakes is also making something called Foxy Lady, a lightly carbonated blush (pink) wine that is a blend of native grapes. In marketing this wine, the Hunts are trying to turn taste on its head, in essence making a virtue out of a defect by promoting the sweet grapey flavor of native wines, which are often disparagingly said to taste "foxy." Soon you will be able to get a T-shirt too: "I'm a Foxy Lady lover." It seems inconceivable that Peter Johnstone, who offers wineglasses etched with herons, would take this tack in his marketing. Derek Wilber, the Hunts' young winemaker, is entirely without apology, though, remarking, "I like to make wines that sell."

Wilber joined the Hunts in 1984. He had been managing

a vineyard, but the opportunity to become a winemaker was irresistible. Wilber admits that at present he is concentrating on the "craft" of wine-making. By that he means mastering engineering, fluid dynamics, refrigeration technology, and chemistry — maintaining the stability of the wines, checking acid and sugar levels. "Right now, I'm making good sound wines, avoiding trouble," he says. A wine-making "style" will come, he believes: deciding whether to adjust the acidity (and therefore fruitiness) of the wine, for example, or whether a Chardonnay is better when aged in casks of oak from Nevers or Limousin, France (Peter Johnstone offers both), and whether the barrels should have a light or a medium "toast" (charring). For the moment, the youthful Wilber says of his young career at a young winery: "At this stage, a lot of it is nuts and bolts."

Mastering the basics is no small accomplishment, certainly not one to be ignored, because, as Wilber notes: "Wine is only a halfway step. The conclusion is vinegar."

When the sommelier pours a splash of wine for the head of the table to sample, he is not asking the patron to approve the choice he made in ordering; he is giving the patron an opportunity to make certain that the wine has not turned. As Wilber says: "Spoilage is the only reason to reject a bottle of wine, and rejection is a serious event."

To prevent that, small wineries use potassium metabisulfite (which releases sulfur dioxide) to stop fermentation at the point desired by the winemaker. (The Food and Drug Administration, which has banned the use of sulfites in salad bars and produce sections of grocery stores, where they had been used to maintain freshness of greens and vegetables, exempted wines from the ban.) Small wineries also use potassium sorbate when bottling sweet wines, to prevent fermentation from starting again in the bottle. The small wineries have no choice but to use these additives; they cannot afford a cold-sterile bottling line, which requires a special filter fine enough to screen out yeast and bacteria from the wine.

The subject of additives makes some wine people uneasy. When diethylene glycol (antifreeze) showed up in Austrian wines overseas, testing in the U.S. then revealed its presence in some Italian wines — Riunite was pulled off store shelves. Deadly levels of methanol — wood alcohol — in cheap Italian wines (not for export) increased public concern. So, as Art Hunt was describing the winemaker's proper chemical repertoire — which may also include cane sugar (to make certain the juice is sweet enough when fermentation begins), chalk (to cut acidity), and bentonite (a clay to eliminate proteins) — Joyce moved uncomfortably in her seat and began to interrupt him. "Art, are you sure . . . ?"

But, in his unaffected way, a man with nothing to hide, Art Hunt just continued to explain how he is adapting so he can make a living. "If you have excellent grapes, then you guide them through the natural process of winemaking," he says. "A winemaker brings out the fine qualities of the grapes."

Other growers are also adapting: one still sells grapes, but also started a trash-hauling business. Another, John Martini, president of the New York State Wine/Grape Growers Association, has cut his vineyard back from 35 acres — the average size for growers in the state — to 21 acres. He has put in 10 acres of French-American hybrids and has also planted plums and apricots. His wife tends the home farm; he manages a Chardonnay and Riesling vineyard.

Martini clearly understands the importance of improving

the image of New York State wines, but he has a broader view of the problem grape growers, winemakers, and wine merchants face: "We're selling all of the wine to ten percent of the people. Let's sell a dinner beverage, something they'll drink in Iowa. Put a screw cap on the bottle so they can put the top back on and stick it in the refrigerator for another night." As if to prove his point, Martini cites figures for average per capita wine consumption: United States, two-and-a-fraction gallons; France, 22 gallons; Italy, 24 gallons, more than ten times the U.S. per capita consumption and more than 8 ounces a day for each Italian.

It is worth noting that *vinifera* grapes account for less than 1 percent of the grapes grown in the state, the French-American hybrids for less than 10 percent. *Fine* wines may boost New York State's image, but *popular* wines are what will make its grape and wine industry flourish.

Almost nothing is forever — sometimes not love itself, and for some, not even the age-old romance of the grape.

"There are an awful lot of romantics in grapes," Jim Moon says, but Moon is not one of them. He used to cultivate twenty acres of grapes as a sideline, but now he makes his money running a motel and selling real estate. "It's better than the grape business," he says knowingly. There is always turnover with 3,400 properties stretched along Keuka Lake's sixty miles of shoreline. Some places are small and modest in price; others are something else again: $315,000 for a house with three hundred feet of shoreline. The vacationers are mostly from New York state, especially Rochester, home of Eastman Kodak, and their cottages are packed along the lakeshore like cracker boxes in a snacker's pantry.

Keuka Lake remains clean enough that more than 95 percent of the lakeshore properties draw their drinking water from it. And the fishing is still good. (Nearby Geneva, New York, which sits at the head of Seneca Lake, proclaims itself "The Lake Trout Capital.") Bill Rutherford, a retired Kodak engineer, says of Keuka, "It's underfished, if anything." Rutherford ought to know. In the summer, he runs the only full-time fishing charter on the lake. Situated south of Branchport, he also operates Port Rutherford, a small marina with rental cabins. Come winter, Rutherford heads to Florida.

Rutherford is evenly tanned with neatly trimmed gray hair. He has a chew of Red Man, and during the conversation, he discreetly brings a glass jar to his mouth and spits quietly. He is a tidy spitter. He sits stiffly, the result of three back operations, and when he moves, he swivels at the waist. Despite his discomfort, he shies from prescription medicines. "I take a lot of aspirin and stay laid down a lot," he says.

Snapshots of successful fisherman cover the corkboard next to the door of his tackle shop. Rutherford logs in every fish caught in his boat, and then enters the data into his computer. His records for the last five years show April and May to be the months to catch big fish. In warm weather, he reports, "big fish take a back seat to large numbers of small fish." Fall is the time to catch landlocked salmon.

To catch fish, Rutherford says you want to have your lines in the water "as soon as it is light enough to read a paper." So we set off at 4:30, before there is any hint of sun above the bluffs to the east of Keuka Lake. Tony and Debbie, who repair gas appliances for a New Jersey utility, are in the boat with us.

Rutherford's twenty-four-foot boat is equipped with sonar that records blips anytime you pass over a fish. It is also equipped with electric down-riggers, weights that take the line to where the fish are, and a submarine speedometer on one down-rigger, so Rutherford can be sure of his trolling speed. Rutherford deftly puts out five lines at different depths, and then we wait, sipping coffee.

The talk is intermittent as Rutherford trolls down one side of the lake for several miles and back up the other side. There are no islands, no coves — the glacier cut a gash, and it has been full of water ever since. "It's like navigating in a bathtub," Rutherford says. We have four strikes. We lose one and haul in three, one decent rainbow trout and two lake trout, one smallish and another respectable, but nothing to write home about, say two pounds. Once they are hooked, we just haul them right in on the ten-pound test line, and they fight about as hard as a size 12 boot might.

Tony and Debbie love to fish — "Debbie is terminally happy," Tony says — and they cannot wait to come back next year. They may not tour the wineries again, though. They did enjoy a visit to Finger Lakes Wine Cellar, but, as Tony reports, "You can get messed up just tasting."

"What did you try?" I ask.

"Everything."

This may be wine and lake country, and some seven million tourists contribute $750 million to the region's economy, but Amos Horning is unlikely to take notice. Amos, sixty-nine, has been working in the fields and is making his way to the kitchen for a late lunch. His face shows no recent acquaintance with a razor. His left boot has a moccasin toe; his right, a plain toe.

Amos, his wife, and their daughter's family moved up from Pennsylvania in 1975, one of the first of eighty-four Mennonite households that have settled in the area. "It's not so full up here," Amos says, explaining why the Mennonites are migrating to the environs of Keuka Lake. And farm prices are a fraction of those in Pennsylvania.

Amos's oldest son, Ivan, moved up with his wife and ten children in the hope of being able to give his sons a start in life. One boy married recently and has set up a shop as a wheelwright. Another son, Nelson, is taking over the family dairy farm, allowing Ivan to return to woodworking, which is the trade he practiced in Pennsylvania. Before Nelson assumed the full burden of his farming duties, he and two friends toured New England on bicycles for two weeks during the summer.

"I'd like to see New England," Ivan says, "but not on a bicycle."

Most Keuka Lake Mennonites travel by horse and black buggy, although a few have cars — painted black, chrome and all. "Black-bumper Mennonites," locals call them, not always kindly. The Keuka Lake Mennonites are more conservative than many of their faith, although they are not so removed from our world as the Amish. The farmers use tractors — which roll on Mennonite-crafted steel tires. Since the steel tires are not allowed on the highways, they "keep the young people on the farm better," Amos says. "They can't take the tractor and run around into town." The Mennonites have two immaculate churches and separate schools for their children, but Ivan chose a farm that sits right on the highway — he knew someday he would want a public spot. He thinks the location will help his woodworking business, and in addition, his wife sells geraniums and bedding plants out of two large greenhouses. She also manages to do a fair lick of laundry: twenty-three pairs of blue jeans hang on the line to dry.

Down a side road, a handmade sign advertises brown eggs for eighty cents a dozen. A young Mennonite farmer is working in the driveway, building a transplanter for vegetable crops. The trays to hold the transplants are bright turquoise, which seems an uncharacteristic color choice for a people whose external trappings are otherwise purposely muted. It happens that the flashy paint was found in the garage when the couple moved into the house two years ago from Pennsylvania — so why not put it to use? The Mennonites have a reputation for being economical — they are said to be the first in line at any local sale of secondhand goods — and in their everyday life, this young couple is giving new meaning to the concept of frugality. The wife, barely out of her teens by the look of her and already the mother of two, heats the laundry water on a homemade stove by burning old asphalt shingles that were recently stripped off the roof.

The young man, in his mid-twenties, is running a diversified farm (although *diversified* is a word he has never heard before): pigs, laying hens, beef cows, oats, and vegetables. I buy a dozen eggs and start talking, without admitting that I am a professional snoop. He is timid, even cautious, but is willing to show me around when I ask for a look. He seems so young and innocent, and already his responsibilities are so great. The stitching in one of his boots is pulling apart at the heel and the insulation is spilling out of holes in his quilted vest. How is everything going? I ask.

"It's a little of a pull," he replies.

The following day I stop by with two fish from Port Rutherford. "How much do you want for them?" he asks as I hand over the fish in a plastic bag.

"Nothing," I tell him, aware even in this gesture that it is futile to imagine that two small fish can swim across the vast gap that separates the farmer and me. His wife, her curiosity having gotten the better of her discretion, peers from a corner of the porch to see what is happening. The farmer gives the fish to his two-and-a-half-year-old son, who carries the bag with the fruit of Keuka Lake to his smiling mother.

"Is your vacation over?" the Mennonite farmer asks.

"Yes," I say. I drive away. I am taking the wine — New York State's and the nation's finest — home with me.

Chapter 7

STRONG DRINK IS RAGING

LYNCHBURG, TENNESSEE — You can't get a headache here. So they say.

I am not talking about the sorts of headaches that come from being laid off from work or from finding that the pigs have slipped through the fence. Such trouble and annoyance are available. What I am talking about is the sort of headache that comes from drinking too much. You know, you wake up in the morning and your mouth feels as though it has been occupied by a fur-bearing mammal and the backs of your eyeballs seem gripped by thumbscrews. Such discomfort, by law, should never greet you in Lynchburg.

That is because, although it is perfectly legal to distill a celebrated sour mash whiskey in Moore County, Tennessee, it is illegal to sell whiskey of any kind. Besides, even if you could buy the local brand, it wouldn't give you a headache.

At least, that is what the folks at the Jack Daniel Distillery here will tell you. The headaches, they insist, "come off the supermarket shelf." It is the impurities in the mixers that do the damage, not their sippin' distillation.

Well, I don't believe the good folks in Lynchburg for a

second on this one. Why should Jack Daniel's be any easier on you the morning after than, say, gin, red wine, or tequila?

Charcoal filtering, they say. It takes two days for the 140-proof alcohol distilled from fermented mash to leach through a ten-foot-high vat packed with pea-sized charcoal. Leaching is alleged to remove the headaches, or, as Roger Brashears, the PR man at the distillery, says, "It takes the hog tracks out."

Perhaps you know the Jack Daniel's advertisements, which to this day still rely on black-and-white photography to convey the idea that the old-time, tried-and-true, slow, craftsman's methods haven't changed in Lynchburg. And if you've seen the ad about making charcoal, you've probably seen Jack Bateman. His picture has been in *Playboy*, and Bateman, a stocky man with dark eyes, tells me that he sometimes receives appreciative letters. He seems to suggest that the attention is hardly surprising, "handsome as I am."

Bateman has been working in the "rickyard" for more than thirty years, and he runs the show there now, making charcoal pretty much the same way he did back when he first came on the job, back when just about everyone's advertisements were in black and white.

The process of making charcoal is simple enough. A crew of about six men operates a small sawmill, ripping hardwood logs into two-by-fours, four feet long. The only acceptable wood is sugar maple. What's more, it is supposed to come from the ridges here in the rolling country of southern Tennessee, not the lowlands. The sticks are stacked six feet high in crisscrossing layers. Four stacks, totaling about two cords, make a "rick," and the ricks are burned one at a time in the open air. The open burning is unconventional, because charcoal is usually made with a fire starved for oxygen, to prevent complete combustion.

A modest amount of art is involved in stacking and burning ricks. The four stacks are placed together and wedged so that they lean toward the middle. The idea is for the rick to collapse into a large heap. A fire is set, the sugar maple blazes away under huge hood, which, if it is working — it wasn't during my visit — combats air pollution. From time to time, Jack Bateman or one of his fellow workers picks up a hose and sprays the fire.

At this stage, the job is not terribly demanding. "All we got around here is time," Bateman remarks. Taking advantage of that commodity, the men stand idly and visit. If, like me, you come from north of the Mason-Dixon line, you'll hardly understand a word they say at first, but it is clear to any casual observer that the conversation here, as at most places where laborers convene, is built on a sturdy foundation of manly insults.

After the rick has collapsed, Bateman occasionally hoses the embers "to knock the ashes off." Once the pile is mostly black coals, one of the men moves in with a scoop shovel and starts shoveling coals into a new pile. All the while, the growing pile is hosed down. From time to time, a fresh man will step in to spell the fellow with the shovel. When the pile has been completely shoveled and hosed, the job is done.

That's how they make charcoal in Lynchburg, the old-fashioned way. It takes time, Jack Bateman warns, his pipe firmly set in his mouth. "You rush the charcoal, you mess up."

While diligently standing around, so as not to rush into

any mistakes, Bateman tries to sell me some real estate. It is a five-acre piece of "level land," he assures me, off which Bateman took 399 bales of hay the previous summer. It is good land, Bateman warrants, and he generously offers me a "good price": $10,000.

"Yeah, a good price for him," Clarence Moorehead, a fellow Jack Daniel's employee, remarks. "You need a boat on it in spring. Don't offer him six thousand, or you'll own it."

Lee Edward ("Billy") Hart owns about 415 acres in four different pieces outside Lynchburg, and some of it is steep hills punctuated by groves of sugar maple, the kind whiskey makers covet for charcoal. Billy is a short man with close-set eyes and a falcon's nose. He makes his living working construction in Tullahoma, to the east of Lynchburg; evenings, he works the farm: 65 head of beef cows, half as many pigs, 20 acres of corn. He rolls up 70 acres of hay into round bales. Billy gets around in a 1963 Ford Fairlane; in the six years he has owned it, he figures he has driven it 100,000 miles. According to Billy, he and his Ford have shared similar lives: "I got a lot of hard miles on me."

Billy and his son, Terry, and his nephew Ronnie, both in their thirties, are going to put on a few more miles before the sun sets this spring afternoon. They're cutting a load of wood for the distillery, where both Terry and Ronnie work doing maintenance. We're heading up a dirt right-of-way to where some of the Harts' cows and pigs graze and the maples stand on a hillside. Terry and Ronnie are in an old truck; Billy and I and Miss Jane, Billy's cheerful wife, ride in a Jeep.

Before we cut any trees, however, the pigs — not unlike humans in their irrepressible desire for freedom — need governing. They have gotten out of their enclosure, but most hang close to the fence. We empty from the vehicles, and all but one are quickly herded back through the gate. Miss Jane calls the independent animal. "Weeweeweewee." He is unimpressed by her serenade.

Terry, with no patience for negotiation, hops in the Jeep, guns it up a hillside to get above the animal, which he drives down through the gate. The rebel pigs corralled, the Harts pile back into their vehicles and head to a shed some three hundred feet away, where the Harts' Russian-made, four-wheel-drive Belarus tractor awaits. Terry tries to get it started, but it will not crank. The stubborn Russian is, however, no match for the polymathic Jeep, which pulls the tractor to life.

Again the clan mounts the vehicles — now Jeep and tractor, which will be used to drag logs — and heads up the big, steep hill, on which, during the remaining hour or so of daylight, we can fell some trees.

"There's no big money in this," Billy informs me on the way up. That is apparent. The Jack Daniel rickyard pays $70 a cord for sugar maple cut to four-foot lengths. The Hart clan will deliver a load of four cords after an evening of felling, an evening of limbing and skidding the logs, an evening of bucking them to length, and an evening of loading them onto their dump truck. First, they must put a new differential in the truck. Still, they will earn $280 that they would not have otherwise, and besides, what better way is there for a family to spend the evenings before planting season?

Up on the hillside, Terry gets his old McCulloch chain saw running; the contingent looks around to choose the first tree to take down. They settle on the largest in the grove. It wants to fall down the hill, but Billy thinks it will be easier to skid out if it falls across the slope. He is determined to see that it is dropped sideways. Terry, in blue jeans and yellow cap with a NAPA label, makes the first cut. Billy then immediately reaches over and grabs the saw from him to start the second cut of the notch. Once he gets the cut headed in a direction that pleases him, he returns the saw to Terry to finish the notch.

Clearly Billy is not a man to leave much to chance — or to anyone else — and the family is obviously used to having him devise the strategy. On the hill above the action, Miss Jane, her oval face framed by gray curls and a kerchief, looks down and smiles.

Billy calls Ronnie to drive an aluminum wedge into the back cut. Ronnie, a husky, bearded man in brown coveralls, leans into the sledge, and the tree lists to Billy's satisfaction. Terry finishes the back cut, and a hundred years of sugar maple topples against its will.

That evening, we down eight large trees, but none as big as the first and none requiring as much of Billy's supervisory talents. Terry and Ronnie, with his own Stihl chain saw, finish limbing the largest tree as dark settles in.

Before supper, a tour of Billy and Miss Jane's place reveals a remarkable array of vehicles, including two homemade dune buggies to take into the hills in winter, two Model A Fords (one elegantly restored), and a stock car. Just how many vehicles do they have in all? Laughter at the question.

Terry: "I don't know."

Miss Jane: "About thirty."

Terry owns an almost equal number of goats. He first got interested in goats as a boy, when it was his job to clear the rocky hillside out back. And what kind of goats are they — milk goats?

"No," Terry replies. "Just goat goats."

"Real brush eaters," Ronnie adds by way of recommendation.

Come supper — dinner is the midday meal, as all good working people in the country know — Terry says good night. His home is the small, one-story brick house a hop, skip down the road past his sister's place. But Ronnie stays on to tuck into Miss Jane's fare: roast pork, boiled potatoes, pinto beans, rolls and cornbread (baked in the shape of corn cobs), green beans, and boiled corn. Dessert is chocolate meringue pie.

And in the worthy tradition of farm wives, Miss Jane gets up twice to refill my glass of iced tea. Her solicitude takes me back to Colorado some fifteen years earlier, when as a hay hand I sat around the table while the Collins women filled the crew's empty glasses almost before they were set back down on the table. I remember those sunny, dusty days, sitting now in this farm kitchen.

Relaxing around Miss Jane and Billy's table, I envy these good people the *society* of the working man's meal. I have enjoyed that, and I am powerfully reminded of it this evening, and I wonder what invisible master lead me to traffic, alone, in words, not, with others, in deeds?

Several days later, feeling lucky to have met the Harts, I say good-bye to Billy and Miss Jane. Before I go, Billy has one thing to say: "That place where we were cutting the sugar maple, that belonged to Miss Jane's father. Miss Jane wanted me to tell you it was the Odis Barlett Farm."

Orval Durm, whose real estate office is located on the main square of Lynchburg, would be happy to sell you such a place. Now is a good time to buy because prices are down. He's got a listing for a 115-acre farm for $75,000. There's probably not much you could do with it. This is a beautiful area, given to great hills with hickory, maple, poplar, and hackberry along the ridges, but there is little level land to plant to crops. In some places, the limestone bedrock juts out, and red cedar seems to thrive everywhere.

Used to be, land in Moore County went for $700 an acre. Today, according to Durm, "Land is two hundred fifty to four hundred dollars an acre, and no takers at that." A lanky man, Durm rises from his seat, crosses a dingy expanse of black-and-white-checked linoleum, and spits tobacco juice into a wastebasket. He gives the impression that he would just as soon spit on the folks running Jack Daniel.

Moore County is one of the smallest counties in the state, but for a spell, more cattle (especially beef and replacement heifers for dairy farms) were raised here than in any other county in Tennessee — thanks to the slop from Jack Daniel. Slop is spent mash, what is left after the soupy mix of grains (80 percent corn, 12 percent rye, and 8 percent barley) has been made into alcohol. Slop is terrific cattle feed, and Jack Daniel sold it to area farmers. The cows got fat, and the farmers maybe put on a layer of reserve also.

Then Jack Daniel did some calculations and figured that it would be more profitable to dry the slop, extracting about half of the grain from the "whole stillage." The company would sell that extracted grain residue separately from the thin stillage that was left. Once drying began, cattle operations were hurt.

There was a time in recent memory when more than 150 farmers were picking up the real slop in their tank trucks. After the slop-drying began, that dropped to about eighty farmers feeding the thin stuff. The cattle business is not as easy or lucrative as it once was, and some operations have gone under. A number of farmers sued Jack Daniel, saying the company promised to keep supplying the real goods. And land prices are down.

Orval Durm, who used to fatten cattle and would like to sell you a piece of land, is disgruntled.

A big part of the problem is that the whiskey business is hurting. For years sales of Jack Daniel's whiskeys kept rising, but through the mid-eighties, they have declined. Back in 1981, when business was booming, Jack Daniel distilled 8 million cases of Tennessee sipping whiskey. They age that in charred oak barrels for at least four years in one of the 46 monolithic warehouses that are a major architectural feature in Lynchburg. Because of the need for aging, the 1981 production did not hit the market until 1986, but sales are off, and the warehouses are full. In 1983, Jack Daniel, seeing the declining trend in liquor sales, cut production to about two million cases. (The cut in production also explains why there is less slop to go around.) In 1986, production went back up, to four million cases, a boost over 1983's output, but still only half of 1981's.

Jack Daniel's problems are industrywide. Sales of beer and wine are off, as are sales of distilled spirits. Only the Kool-Aid of the liquor industry, the alcoholic equivalent of bubble gum — the wine cooler — is running counter to the trend. Among the boozes of choice, Jack Daniel's Tennessee Whiskey remains among the top six or eight, behind such notables as Smirnoff vodka, Baccardi rum, Jim Beam bourbon, Seagram's 7 Crown, and Canadian Mist.

Canadian Mist, as it happens, is owned by Brown-Forman Distillers, the same company that bought privately held Jack Daniel back in the mid-fifties. This absentee ownership is a hotter topic today than it was a few years ago — no doubt because of the layoffs.

With production cut, Jack Daniel simply did not need as many employees as it once did. Hence, two hundred people received pink slips. What happened, though, was not that simple. A number of layoffs came around the holiday season, so some people were dismissed one day and then, almost the next, were offered jobs — as seasonal employees — at a big cut in pay ($3 per hour) and with no benefits.

Bosses, or, to use the jargon of the day, managers, engage in such cold-blooded conduct under the guise of being businesslike. What that means is that the bosses miscalculate and people below them pay. Alas, such is the nature of the workplace, expediency and fear masquerade as efficiency. This charade causes bad blood, and in Lynchburg, the Steelworkers Union moved in to try to organize the workers. They failed, being defeated by a vote of 146 to 96.

An organizer from the Steelworkers Union notes, however, "Once management starts treating people the way it has recently, it never changes back for the good. Jack Daniel will eventually have a union." So far, that prediction has proven to be no more than wishful thinking. Management's response is to say the fault is yours and mine: they had to pare employees because you and I are no longer sipping as much Tennessee whiskey.

Brother Don Burkhalter admits he drinks, but nothing more than wine at communion. Brother Don is the preacher at the Arbor Primitive Baptist Church in Lynchburg, and some of his brethren work at Jack Daniel. "I preach the Bible," Brother Don says. "I preach on alcohol," he adds, and then quotes Proverbs 20:1, "Wine is a mocker, strong drink is raging."

Ten years ago, the congregation of Arbor Primitive invited Brother Don up from Alabama, where he was both working in sales for a linen company and, because he had the calling, preaching on the side. At the time when he took over Arbor Primitive, about forty people attended services. Now, one hundred forty take their places in the modest brick church.

Mankind has abiding spiritual needs, and life's meaning is explored in many temples, surrogates like health spas and pyschiatrists' consulting rooms, but in Lynchburg, the townsfolk appear to rely on the traditional vehicle. More than twenty churches, many either Baptist or Church of Christ, provide for the county's 4,510 residents. Brother Don says that almost everyone he knows attends church.

He and his family live in a new four-thousand-square-foot "California Contemporary"–style house. Inside, the color television is on, fed an extraordinary diet of shows by a satellite dish. "You can get about a hundred and thirty-five stations," Brother Don tells me. As he reports this, reruns of "The Jetsons" are being beamed on-screen.

When he arrived in Lynchburg, Brother Don parted his blond hair on the side. Now, his hair is swept back and falls in a curl over his shirt collar. He favors blue jeans, cowboy boots in a gray reptilian pattern, and cologne. In his early forties, he seems smooth for a humble servant of the Lord. Or, as one townsman said, "He's kinda hip for a preacher."

Brother Don, for his part, acknowledges, "I'm different from most preachers." He certainly does not resemble the black-suited, backward-collared clerics of my Episcopalian but irreligious youth, and I recognize in myself an inclination to make light of him because he is not what I grew up knowing. "I just try to be a part of the community," he says.

He appears to have been successful. Arbor Baptist has the largest youth group in the county. Brother Don and his wife, Sara, a schoolteacher in Lynchburg, have two daughters. They are also part of a special foster parents' program and have taken in a girl whose life has had more than its fair share of unhappiness. If I find myself edging toward disrespect for a man of God who sits around with cartoons on his television set, I find that derision counterweighted by regard for this man who is clearly devoting a substantial part of himself to God's literal children. Under the tutelage of Sara, the Sunshine Kids, a youthful contingent at Arbor Primitive, has recorded two albums and carried their singing ministry through the South.

Brother Don himself has traveled to speak at revivals, and he conveys the impression of a man who enjoys the limelight. For now, though, he studies the Bible and visits the sick and shut-in. He does not, however, visit women his own age during the day. That could set tongues to wagging, and he explains, "The quickest way to get the church is to get its head."

And who would want to get the church? I wonder. Without hesitation, Brother Don responds: "Satan would."

The two-story brick county courthouse sits in the center of Lynchburg's town square. Stores surround it: the farmer's co-op, the bank, Orval Durm's office, a small grocery, a pharmacy, the Iron Kettle (breakfast and lunch only). The paint store stands empty. In the window, a cardboard sign reads:

> Ever
> thing
> 50%
> off.

Jack Daniel owns several stores on the square, including the Lynchburg Hardware & General Store. It is actually a tourist trap. Offering an array of souvenirs, it operates with a predictable, wink-and-a-nod, aren't-we-hillbillies humor, advertising black denim overalls as Tennessee Deluxe Tux and selling the well-known caps: Jack Daniel's Field Tester and Jack Daniel's–Lynchburg Lemonade. The store also sells monogrammed everything: shot glasses, shirts, golf balls, and belt buckles.

About 300,000 people tour the distillery annually, and that is a lot of traffic for a little town of 672 souls. Some, of course, resent the congestion: "I guess the tourists think Jack Daniel owns the town," is how Orval Durm put it.

One clerk in the courthouse remarked, as do people in any community plagued by pushy tourists (is there any other kind?): "I liked it better when they didn't let foreigners in, and if they did, they run 'em out at sundown. That was when we had enough trees to hang folks from." Remember, we are in Lynchburg.

Some townsfolk in Lynchburg will make sure you understand that Jack Daniel isn't just a bunch of good ole boys, whistlin' and spittin' and making white lightnin'. "There's a little ill will since Jack Daniel has been took over by outsiders," Orval Durm says.

"Jews," confides a man of the cloth, who leans close when he says this in a knowing tone that betrays no kindness.

But Brown-Forman in Louisville, Kentucky, bought the company from Jack Daniel's descendants more than thirty years ago, and Brown-Forman, whose stock is traded on the American Stock Exchange, has some ten thousand shareholders. Durm and the anti-Semitic preacher and anyone else in town could pick up the stock for themselves. Everyone in Lynchburg understands that outsiders own the distillery; few seem to understand just how many absentee owners there are, although they find it convenient to blame them nonetheless.

Things may have seemed better when Lem Motlow, Jack Daniel's nephew, was in charge, or when Mr. Lem's four sons were at the helm. But in and around Lynchburg, you'll find people who had to leave the area years ago to make a living. In old age, they have returned to wind down their final years and perhaps even be buried in the family plot in the same hillside cemetery that is home to Jack Daniel's abbreviated bones. (A short man, Jack kicked a recalcitrant safe late in life, leading to the amputation of his toe, and then his leg, in two parts, before he died of gangrene.)

Life in Moore County may be uncertain today, but when wasn't it? People may have felt more secure with a couple of Motlows living in big houses and running things; there is a comfort in knowing local folks are boss, but local ownership does not provide any guarantees. It may seem inconceivable that Mr. Lem, who knew your pappy before you, wouldn't give you a square deal, but he also probably was not offering a starting wage of $9.54 an hour, with generous benefits.

The paternalism — or feudalism — of the old days has gone, and if that change is not unsettling enough, the liquor business has hit a bad patch. The grumbling should come as no surprise. "Outside management" is a convenient scapegoat — I suspect we have all heard it blamed in more sophisticated places than Lynchburg.

Still, Lynchburg is a homey place. It is a county seat without a lawyer practicing in town. It is a place, like small places everywhere, that would like to have hung onto what it most treasured about its past while being blessed by the benefits of modern times — Daddy Lem guarding over, while we all earned enough to buy satellite dishes.

Sheriff Herb Glassmeyer, a balding former highway patrolman in his forties, has been a cop since he was twenty-three. "Really, that's all I know," he says. "I like people; that's why I'm in this. Policemen feel like they're doing a service."

And sometimes when things go wrong, Herb Glassmeyer steps in: "Sometimes I feel like I'm helping the situation. I feel like I'm worthwhile." That is about as straightforward and fundamental an assessment of human value as you can get.

Later, while describing his job, Glassmeyer discusses the dangers a solitary small-town lawman faces, and, in doing so, the sheriff offers up another fundamental principle, this time of the life in Moore County or in small places everywhere. "It takes a certain kind of person to handle the situation. We don't ride in pairs, so when you go into a tight spot, there's no backup. It's root, hog — or die."

Chapter 8

FIGHTING THE COLD

INTERNATIONAL FALLS, MINNESOTA — Manny's bulldozer has broken through the ice. Don Carroll hears the news at 3:30 P.M., after returning to headquarters in the Falls following a day of checking the haul roads through Boise Cascade's woodlands. Carroll, a Boise Cascade forester, is responsible for the maintenance of some 300 miles of woods roads that run through the 304,000 acres of forest that Boise, the largest private landowner in the state, manages in northeastern Minnesota. With the arrival of winter, it is crucial that roads through the boggy northland be frozen and cleared so that pulpwood can be trucked out. The Boise Cascade paper mill in International Falls requires 275,000 cords of pulpwood a year, a cord being 128 cubic feet of wood, the equivalent of a stack four feet wide, by four feet high, by eight feet long. About 40 percent of the wood for the paper mill is cut and trucked during a three-month stretch during the winter, when the frozen roads are able to support the heavy logging equipment and pulpwood trucks. For Don Carroll, with the major cutting season just underway, a sinking bulldozer 50 miles to the south is a problem in need of immediate solution.

From what he has heard over the CB radio, Carroll knows he needs a winch. Manny's own winch rests underwater, and Manny's partner, Jack, snapped the three-quarter-inch cable on his bulldozer trying to fish Manny out. Carroll speaks with Boise's head mechanic, Dave Backlund, and arranges to have him truck a Bombardier to the accident site. The Bombardier, a small, relatively lightweight crawler, with wide rubber tracks and steel cleats, can tread where a heavier 'dozer cannot, and it has a winch mounted behind. Carroll fetches a spare length of cable for Jack's winch and rounds up miscellaneous supplies: flashlight batteries, a length of chain, and a large hook and a snatch block.

By the time he starts south at 4:30, it is dark. Jim Hebner, the supervisor of Boise's foresters, gets on the radio. He has just spoken with Manny and Jack and heard worry in their voices. "You probably should get some groceries," he advises Carroll. "It could be a long night."

On the way out of town, Carroll stops by his house and picks up a heavy coat and woolen pants — it has been known to get cold in these parts, though, as Manny's predicament suggests, it hasn't been cold enough to get a good foundation of ice on the streams running through the woods roads. Then Carroll stocks up at a convenience store. His groceries consist of a box of doughnuts, six half-pints of milk, five Cokes, three Milky Ways, and two Three Musketeers.

After almost an hour and a half of driving, the last eleven miles of it on a rough, snow-covered haul road, Carroll, with Backlund close behind, pulls into sight of Manny and Jack, who have been joined by the Boise forester responsible for this section of woodland. They lead Carroll up the road to the spot where Manny's machine has broken through the three-inch-thick ice; half of the rear and the better portion of the right tread are underwater. As the Boise Cascade crew calculates how to extricate the machine, the sixteen-ton D-6 Cat sits immobile in the dark.

Then Backlund takes over. He drives the Bombardier off the trailer and tiptoes it across a narrow stretch of ice, after which he bushwhacks through some brush, coming to rest fifty feet to the left of the bulldozer. He attaches the Bombardier's winch cable to the 'dozer, while Manny scrambles up onto the 'dozer's left track and into his accustomed seat behind the controls. Both Manny and Backlund crank up their engines, and Backlund starts the Bombardier's winch cranking. Spectators move quickly to take cover behind trees — a snapping cable could sever a limb.

The cable tightens; the winch grates and squeals, and Manny's 'dozer begins to rise out of its watery hole. Manny has locked his left track, which is resting on the thin ice, and he lets the partially submerged right track turn with the hope that it will get a purchase on the ice and spin the bulldozer toward the Bombardier. It seems a reasonable plan, and if there is a man to execute it, Manny is the one. As Don Carroll says of him, "He's one of the best Cat skinners in the Northland — he can walk a Cat across lily pads." But he cannot make it breach like a whale — at least not tonight.

Suddenly the squealing of the winch changes octaves, rising shrilly like a goosed soprano, and Backlund quickly shuts the Bombardier down. The universal joint is shot — time to modify the leverage.

The crew decides to slip the spare three-quarter-inch cable into a snatch block affixed to the Bombardier's winch cable, about halfway between the Bombardier and Manny's

Cat. They run the three-quarter-inch cable onto the winch on Jack's D-6 Cat and see if it has the snort to finish hoisting Manny out. After ten minutes of setting things up, plunging bare hands into the snow to find a nut that was dropped, checking attachments, making adjustments, the men are ready to roll. Manny sits atop his listing machine, and Jack sits atop his 'dozer a hundred feet away. Everyone else is ducking behind the biggest trees they can find.

And in thirty seconds, it is all over. Manny is rescued, an uncommon problem quickly solved, another small, anticlimactic, everyday drama ended. Don Carroll breaks out the doughnuts and milk.

"That's a pretty hostile environment out there," the John Deere specialist in forest products says of the Minnesota timber country.

"There's nothin' that don't break in the woods," Glen Wright, twenty-seven, says. He should know: that morning he had snapped off one of the hydraulic fingers on his John Deere 743 feller-buncher. This wood-harvesting machine is a hybrid that combines the articulated frame and protected cab of a 150-horsepower skidder with a standard backhoe boom, on which is attached a cutting head — stainless-steel shears capable of generating 99,000 pounds of cutting force, enough to snip an aspen tree 22 inches in diameter.

There are few trees in the North Woods that Wright's clippers cannot handle, and his family operation is typical of the seventy-five or so logging outfits cutting under contract to Boise. While Wright is falling — they don't say "felling" in these parts — as many as four or five trees a minute, his brother-in-law is running a skidder with a grapple, a large hydraulic clamp off the back of the skidder that grabs the butt ends of downed trees. This $85,000 machine is capable of handling a cord or more of tree-length poles in each load. Wright's father is driving the logging truck; each truckload, which contains about ten cords of poles, is worth approximately $350 each, the price varying with the distance logs have to be hauled and with the species — black spruce being more valuable than aspen. Working around the landing, where the tree-length poles are piled before being loaded onto the truck, is a fourth member of the crew. He is using a chain saw to limb the trees and cut off the tops. As Glen Wright's father loads poles on his truck with a hydraulic boom, his junior partner — without safety glasses, hearing protection, or hard hat — works under the boom with a chain saw. "You seldom see a guy in northern Minnesota wearing the protection he should," Don Carroll remarks. Or, to put this foolishness another way, men will be boys.

Wright is clear-cutting a forty-acre block, one of four he is under contract to cut for Boise. The entire cut will yield approximately 4,000 cords of pulpwood, and the cutting will be completed by the spring thaw. It has to be, since the ground is impossible in warm weather. Fortunately, though, the winters here are long and deep.

But let's get the facts straight: *It is not the coldest place in the United States.*

Max Glime, a meteorological technician at the International Falls weather station since 1956, alleges: "We have the coldest temperature more often than anyplace else." But the record proves him wrong.

According to David Hickcox, a professor at Ohio Wesleyan University who keeps track of such data, in 1987, West Yellowstone, Montana, recorded the nation's daily low temperature on eighty days; International Falls had the daily low only seventeen days, *sixth* on the list of cold places. In 1985 and 1986, Gunnison, Colorado, had more daily lows than any other location, 74 times in 1985 and 81 times in 1986. By contrast, International Falls was tied for fifth on the list in 1985 with thirteen low days, and sixth on the list in 1986 with eleven low days. In addition to Gunnison and West Yellowstone, Truckee, California, Houlton, Maine, and Marquette, Michigan, all had more national daily lows in 1986.

But let's give the Falls its due: in 1987, it did have the coldest temperature recorded anywhere in the Lower Fortyeight, −38°F, on January 7.

David Ludlum, a weather historian, remains unimpressed: "There are a lot colder places in North Dakota." The coldest winter on record, for example, was the winter of 1935–1936 in Langdon, North Dakota, where the average temperature was −8.4°F. The town had sixty-seven consecutive days when the minimum temperature was below zero, and — catch this — forty-one consecutive days when the daily high was below zero.

International Falls is proud of its cold weather nonetheless, and the state legislature has provided the city with $700,000 to develop a cold-weather testing facility. Jaguar, Rolls-Royce, and other European auto makers routinely bring their new models here in the winter to test them against the elements, making a track on the ice on Rainey Lake and driving round the clock.

The town even plans to boast a little about its cold by

erecting a giant thermometer in the middle of town, providing some statuesque competition for Smokey the Bear, patron saint of forests, who has loomed over the park.

Much of the land south and west of International Falls is old glacial lake bed. Lake Agassiz, which extended from northern Canada into this area, was in its time larger than all the Great Lakes combined. Much of that and other ancient lake beds are now filled with peat up to fifteen feet deep, and the land, if you can call it that, is a spongy mat. The area south of the Falls is part of the second largest muskeg swamp in the world; the largest is in the Soviet Union. Black spruce and tamarack grow in the bogs. The high ground mostly grows quaking aspen, or "popple," as it is commonly called.

Also found on the drier high spots is black ash (a hardwood, prized for firewood), balm of Gilead (pronounced "bam"), and Norway (or red) pine, the state tree.

"High ground" is a relative term. From a forester's point of view, an elevation of a mere foot or two qualifies as upland here. According to Alan Ek, chairman of the Department of Forestry at the University of Minnesota, a difference of four inches in elevation in a bog makes a significant difference in how well black spruce will grow.

For the loggers to be able to get onto the spongy ground, the roads must be tended. Sometime around Thanksgiving, the cold begins to roll in, and Don Carroll sends Manny and Jack out in the Bombardiers to pack the snow on the haul roads so they will freeze more quickly. The big Cats follow, as Carroll and his crew work to push the frost into the ground.

The loggers follow, but not as many as a decade ago. Although the mechanization of the forest around International Falls is modest by the standards of, say, northern Ontario, still, according to Don Carroll, "What used to take a week to accomplish when I started in 1973 now takes an hour." Glen Wright's four-man crew will take out close to a hundred cords of wood a day.

The trees are harvested when they are "economically mature," in the words of one University of Minnesota extension forester. For aspen, that means between forty and fifty years old; for black spruce, about eighty years old.

The sites are clear-cut, forty acres being about as large an areas as is harvested at one time. Several considerations limit the size of a cut. The most obvious is the acreage of the stand of ripe timber. Erosion is not a concern, given the flat terrain, but regeneration is. Aspen send their new shoots up from their roots, but for spruce to return, there must be a source of seeds nearby. If a spruce clearcut is too large, natural reseeding will be light. Moreover, excess water can hinder germination, and if too many trees are removed from any one area, reduced transpiration from the loss of trees can lead to a rise in the water table. As Paul Jensen, who heads Boise's woodlands division, said, "The trees just suck the moisture right out of the ground." If too large a block of trees is removed, all that water just sits there.

According to Ek of the University of Minnesota, "The people at Boise have tended to be rather good and careful stewards of the forest," but the simple truth is, the industrial forest is monotonous. The majesty of the legendary North Woods is not to be found here. As Ek explains, "The better sites feed the pulp and paper industry," which means that the woods resemble any intensively managed cropland. The woods are farmed, the cellulose stalks mowed on forty- and eighty-year rotations, and the methods here, like those in agriculture, have evolved with expensive machinery replacing manpower. The logging camp is history. The appetite of the paper mill does not allow for the patient encouragement of white and Norway pine for sawlogs for lumber; with only a two-and-a-half-month growing season this far north, they would take more than a century to reach marketable size. There is no magic in the woods; they have been reduced to a mere resource, the raw material for photocopier paper and bumper stickers.

The Boise Cascade paper mill in International Falls makes 575 tons of paper a day; it runs all year round and round the clock, producing a total of 208,000 tons of envelopes, photocopier paper, and coated backing for bumper stickers. Some 9,000 people live in this isolated city set on the Rainy River, the border between the United States and Canada, 300 miles north of Minneapolis–Saint Paul. The mill employs 750, paying out $32 million annually in payroll. For years, Boise Cascade and International Falls have been synonymous — indeed, in the mid-eighties Boise employed another 550 people in the Falls and had another 100 loggers providing the company with an additional 150,000 cords of wood.

But then one day — December 6, 1984, to be precise — Boise shut down its unprofitable Insulite plant, which made fiberboard sheathing and siding, notifying workers in the morning that the plant would close for good that afternoon. Workers in International Falls had been making brand-named Bild-Rite and Gray-Lite since 1911, but on the forty-third anniversary of Pearl Harbor, history's most famous sneak attack, the city of International Falls relearned the lesson that many forget and that is always painful to rediscover: there is no such thing as security in this life. Even large corporations paying handsome wages with generous benefits leave workers, sometimes unionized workers, out in the cold — a statement to be taken literally in northern Minnesota.

Jim Sether was working at the Insulite plant at the time of the closing. A longtime Boise employee, a shop steward, and a member of his union's grievance committee, Sether says of the closing, "It was like a death of a whole family. But it kicked complacency in the ass."

Bob Schwiderski was brought into the Falls after the closing of the Insulite plant as the city's director of economic development. His job is to help the town get back on its business feet. "The people have to realize that Boise can no longer be the benefactor of the whole community," he says. "They have to realize that there's more than one way to get a job."

Chronologically not yet forty, Schwiderski says, "My stomach is fifty." A heavy smoker, he is struggling to quit, a promise he made to Frank Orsi, a Canadian businessman who, in part because of Schwiderski's courtship of him, is reopening the Insulite plant at a new location in the Falls. Plans call for fifty workers to be hired, and if economic projections are accurate, when the reborn operation is going full steam, it will pay some $3.4 million in salaries — split evenly between factory workers and loggers supplying wood chips. The town will also be a beneficiary of the revivified plant; it will receive some $180,000 annually in real estate taxes.

But the fact is, the Orsi plant will not pay the kind of wages that the Boise Cascade paper mill pays. Boise's 615 hourly workers are represented by nine different unions — including woodworkers, paperworkers, electricians, teamsters, and pipefitters. Orsi does not plan to run a union shop, which means that he will not be paying union wages. With the town in need of jobs, no one is grumbling publicly.

"People see International Falls as a hard-nosed union town, but no one in this town is going to shove a union down Orsi's throat," promises Jim Sether, a substantial man who says disc problems have shrunk him almost two inches from the six feet five inches he stood in his prime. Sether, who is collecting more than $300 a month in workmen's compensation for a variety of work-related injuries, adds, "As Bob Walls [president of the joint union council] says, 'Unions are not born, they are caused.' "

To which a doubtful Schwiderski interjects: "They are a part of the social fabric of the Falls." That fabric was rent by Boise's closing of the Insulite plant — might Orsi's mending lead to a new pattern in town? Schwiderski is cautious, but hopeful: "Let's give the new business a chance."

International Falls makes its money off the area's natural bounty, even when that does not mean cutting down trees.

Evelyn Henrickson is dressed in a pin-striped suit. Trim, dark-haired, mid-fortyish, she is the wife of a bank president and executive director of the Chamber of Commerce. She works out of a basement office in the new building the Chamber shares with a state travel information center. Although summer people have always ventured to the lake country of northern Minnesota, International Falls has never made a concerted effort to draw them. In fact, many residents were just as happy when the tourists kept right on going across the bridge into Canada. As Henrickson says, "We have a small-town atmosphere. You get a little provincialism where there's an unwillingness to share. People say, 'I don't want anybody standing in front of me at the fast-food joint.' Now they know that they have to put up with that for the good of the community."

For the *economic* good, I should note, which is not synonymous with other goods — social, spiritual, and environmental, to mention three.

The Falls' big publicity push is to broadcast the existence of Voyageurs National Park to unsuspecting water lovers everywhere. The park is on the historic route of the voyageurs — stubby, stout-hearted, canoe-paddling French-Canadian fur traders. It was created in 1975 and contains 344 square miles and four major lakes within its boundaries to the east and south of town. "The park is the world's best-kept secret," Schwiderski says — to the dismay of its promoters in the Falls. Unlike the Boundary Waters Canoe Area farther to the east, the park does not prohibit the use of motors — in fact, it has some hundred mooring sites for houseboats, the waterborne equivalent of Winnebagos. These vessels are, in the words of Henrickson, "top shelf. They have all the comforts of home: shower, bath, kitchen." Such is the Wilderness Experience today. "If it rains, you can be inside."

Bob Anderson, former mayor of the Falls and now communications manager for the paper mill, says "For a long time, people wanted to keep Rainy Lake and the natural resources — the hunting and the fishing — to themselves. They didn't want outsiders to come here, but the outsiders keep the businessmen in business."

One laid-off Boise worker and disgruntled former union man has his doubts: "Tourism is not going to support the people who live here. Tourism is seasonal and minimum-wage." Economics aside, the union man makes no effort to disguise his contempt for the visitors: "The people here go fishing in Canada. We know the lakes that are untouched. The tourists never find them."

For those like the unemployed union man, the whole idea of accommodating tourists is anathema. Pleasing vacationers is, along with prostitution, the ultimate service occupation. The tourist is looking for a good time, and may pay a tidy sum to get it — then again, he or she may not. Not everyone has a deferential nature, a willingness to put a stranger's needs and pleasures ahead of one's own. Evelyn Henrickson says she just wants to try to get the northward-bound vacationers to stop, however briefly, on the U.S. side of the river. "I want International Falls to stop being simply a passage to Canada," she says. Unfortunately, the attitude required of those who would turn a buck in the tourist hustle is not necessarily what you are likely to find among people living in a remote town with a harsh climate.

International Falls is a white-bread town. It produced the legendary Cleveland Browns fullback Bronko Nagurski and the famed makeup artist Tammy Faye Bakker. Third Street looks like Main Streets all over the Midwest: it is wide, with flat-roofed two- and three-story brick buildings that run for a stretch of several blocks. Most of the residences are one-

story wood-frame houses with wide horizontal siding —
Boise siding, pressed fiberboard with a vinyl paint bonded
to it.

In other words, this is not a town in which to run a
health-food store or practice as an architect, although James
Cowgill has tried to make a living doing both since moving
up here twelve years ago from Minneapolis with his wife
and daughter. Their "Organic Gourmet" sold health foods
and cookware. "It did not do very well," Cowgill admits.
"We lost money for two or three years and gave it up."

He is still a practicing architect, although he says, "If you
were to do every new building in town, you'd never make
a living." He has designed the new airport terminal, a lo-
comotive roundhouse for Boise, a combination liquor store
and gas station, the new travel information center (housing
the Chamber of Commerce's offices) and a number of
houses, mostly summer places on Rainy Lake to the east of
town. Cowgill comments on his houses: "People will say,
'Cowgill did that,' because it has real wood siding on it."

In his gray flannel slacks, maroon crew-neck sweater,
and wire-rimmed glasses, Cowgill looks different from most
people in town — more polished, even in informal attire.
Beneath his office right on the river in Ranier, a couple of
miles east of the Falls, he has a small art gallery and framing
business, and next to that, he sells pottery. "About a
hundred people shop here and use my services," he says.
"It's difficult to make a living, but we enjoy Rainy Lake and
the area."

Like many highly trained exurbanites in small places all
over, Cowgill is something of an outsider in his adopted
home — and he is torn between his affection for his chosen
spot and the limited cultural opportunities. "The thing that

concerns me," he says, "living here as long as we have, is that I not lose my perspective about what's going on — not just architecturally."

One way to fight insularity is to bring in new blood. Koochiching County, home to the Falls, lost about 2,000 residents during the eighties. It was down to 15,700 inhabitants in its two million acres, but some considerable time after my stay in the Falls, two unrelated developments seemed to offer the hope that prospects would pick up.

First, county officials thought to lure newcomers by giving homesteading another chance. They offered forty acres to anyone who would come up north, build a house, and live in it for ten years. The newcomers had to start with one basic qualification: "We want people that are self-sufficient," Schwiderski said, meaning they should bring their means of support with them. The homesteaders' parcels would come from land that had passed into the county's hands when previous landowners defaulted on taxes.

Picked up by the press, the program prompted some 3,500 applications; the county authorized the awarding of one hundred homesteads. Perhaps the Falls would not get a major transfusion of new talent, but there was some fresh blood.

Second, Boise Cascade is investing $525 million upgrading the mill. With some two thousand construction workers on the job — many of them from out of town and out of state, the Falls is enjoying a boom during construction. It is worth noting, however, that the construction contract was awarded to a nonunion firm in Atlanta. Following confrontations between Boise's union employees and nonunion construction workers, riots ensued. No deaths resulted, but personal injury and property destruction did. (As an aside, the fiberboard plant has continued to operate as an open shop, although a vote is scheduled to see whether the workers there will seek union representation.)

What the expansion means is that Boise is putting in a state-of-the-art paper-making machine, which will increase the mill's capacity. This "expansion," as it is being called, does not, however, necessarily mean more jobs. Initially sixty to seventy jobs will be created when the new machine starts humming, but that increase could eventually be more than offset by the idling of older equipment in the mill. Such is the speculation.

A half-billion-dollar investment is nothing to sneer at, but it basically means a reprieve for the Falls. The mill will be made competitive; it will not be phased out while some new plant is located elsewhere, the Pacific Rim even, where labor is cheap. In effect, a down-on-its-luck burg gets a rematch. International Falls will have a chance to keep slugging it out. In this life, you can't ask for more than that.

Chapter 9

THE TOWN THE RAIN MADE

SOLDIERS GROVE, WISCONSIN — In this unique town, you can tell a lot about a person by his views on the sunset. I refer not to judgments about its beauty, whether a burnt umber sky is more lovely and moving than a salmon-colored dusk fading to dusty rose. Rather I refer simply to the hour at which the sun goes behind the hills. That time is crucial in this town in southwestern Wisconsin because Soldiers Grove is the nation's first — and only — solar village. So when the winter sun goes down, the heat goes off.

The grumblers and complainers, of which there are a fair number hereabouts, say the sun sets at 2 P.M. on a midwinter afternoon. Those of a positive cast will tell you that the sun sets closer to 3 P.M. That disparity in views is revealing.

The fact is that if you are standing at the entrance to Cecil Turk's solar-heated IGA, the sun sets before 2 P.M. on December 21, the shortest day of the year. That is early, and explaining why there is a solar IGA at all in Soldiers Grove, why it fails to get the afternoon sun, and why people dispute the time of sunset, all requires some history. That history will be simplified here so we can get back to Cecil Turk, standing proudly in front of his new store, near the entrance to town on the main drag, named Passive-Solar Drive. In 1857, Joseph Brightman built his sawmill on the Kickapoo River. That grew into the town of Soldiers Grove, whose commercial center was, until the mid-eighties, tucked in a meander of the river. When the river got high, Soldiers Grove got wet — a clear causal relationship. Flood damages came to an annual average of $127,000.

Geography is destiny. Government projects throughout the land have been dedicated to the refutation of that truth, however, and the engineers have won some battles — temporarily, anyway. For example, millions of people now live in the once arid Southwest because of the creation of an enormous federal tap that enables them to draw cheap water, water never meant for their desert homes. And inversely, the city of New Orleans remains dry because of diversions, levees, and other technological legerdemain. Indeed, people all over this country live where high water should by nature run, except that the Army Corps of Engineers has dammed a river or straightened its course or dug its channel deeper or built its banks higher, or done all four. The corps, dedicated to the proposition that the technician is omnipotent, that geography is malleable, that rivers can be made into rain gutters, has spent billions of dollars on flood control. Yet still the waters spill their banks. Back in the 1970s, the corps had its chiropractic eye on the Kickapoo — another riverine spine to be manipulated.

Soldiers Grove was a sick town, probably terminal. Because of flooding, Highway 61 had been routed around the town back in the 1950s. Now the population was down, and of those who remained, many were elderly (this, a familiar aspect of rural small towns), and more than a third of the residents earned less than $3,000 (this, at a time when that seemed the prevailing hourly wage on Wall Street). The town had no choice but to pass flood-plain zoning — or face the cutoff of federal and state funds and, ultimately, bank credit.

The corps had proposed a flood-control dam upriver, and along the banks of the river in Soldiers Grove, a levee, this latter at a mere $3.5 million, to protect property in town — 39 businesses and 22 residences — worth about $1 million. But prospects for construction of the upstream LaFarge dam were dim, given various challenges to it, and the levee's cost to the town was more than the townspeople could reasonably bear — $10,000 annually for upkeep in a town that at the time collected $14,000 in taxes a year. Another solution was necessary. Although the corps had dismissed lock-stock-and-barrel relocation of the flood-plain properties as "socially unacceptable," the town pressed the corps to study that possibility anyway. The corps agreed, but soon afterward, the whole Kickapoo Valley project was called to a halt, and the corps pulled out — no levee and no help with relocation. The town pressed ahead on its own, hired a graduate student as its relocation coordinator, and, in June of 1977, some two years after the corps' retreat, the town invested 90,000 of its own dollars to purchase 200 acres on Highway 61 for a new townsite.

As it passes through Soldiers Grove, the Kickapoo is a quiet fifty-foot-wide river of brown water flowing slowly ten feet below its banks. It is difficult to conceive of it as having been a threat to the town, of being a force that requires more than $3 million to tame. But this is the so-called "driftless area" of Wisconsin, the part of the state that was not covered by glaciers during the last Ice Age. It is up-and-down land — with maple and birch on the hillsides and as pretty country as you'll see anywhere — given to small dairy herds and modest plots of tobacco. (The tobacco used to be grown for cigar wrappers, but its "drinkability" — capacity to absorb its weight in, say, molasses — makes it a favorite for chewing.) When it rains in this hill country, the water pours down off the slopes, filling the feeder streams in the low ground; they then run fast into the Kickapoo.

In late June of 1978, the rain came. The Kickapoo watershed got soaked, and water sluiced off the steep ground in sheets and turned the gentle river ugly. After the storm, which resulted in the worst flood in the town's history, causing half a million dollars' damage, folks in Soldiers Grove told disaster-relief officials it was time to move the town. And not just move it, but make it solar.

What immediately comes to mind when someone mentions the nation's first solar village? A hip place in California, perhaps. Maybe Buckminster Fuller adherents in the high, sunny country of New Mexico. Chances are you do not think of a town on the solar cutting edge as one that is cloudy, poor, and almost half pensioners. To tell the truth, lots of folks here didn't see their town that way either.

A one-time confluence of events — including an energy crisis and a flood — available money, and people, some no longer around, caused this anomalous village to spring up. Various legends have it that different people first proposed the idea that the new village be solar-heated. The town leaders were looking for a theme, an image, to give the relocation project an identity — a Wild West motif was suggested and discarded, for example. But this is the upper Midwest, which means no one is surprised when the temperature hits thirty below zero in the winter, and at the time, oil was pushing $30 a barrel. So no matter who first propounded the notion of a sun-centered reincarnation, the idea won supporters, not the least of whom was Tom Hirsch, a former back-to-the-lander who now works for the state.

Hirsch was hired as the town's relocation coordinator. As he says, "We were building for the future." And with "guts and preseverance," as another participant put it, Soldiers Grove was remade.

It cost the town government about $2 million and the federal and state governments some $4 million. The many deals weren't put together easily, but the vitality was there to put them together, and Cecil Turk, who was president of the village trustees when the relocation request was first made to federal officials, was soon to have his sun-blessed grocery — in front of which we left him standing a couple of pages ago.

Does solar heating work in Soldiers Grove?

"When the sun shines," several people replied. They weren't simply stating the obvious, they were expressing their abiding skepticism. Wisconsin is not the searing Southwest; it receives only 45 percent of the possible sunshine in December, the cloudiest month. Skeptics know that more than half of the days are cloudy. Skeptics and proponents alike know that the site of the new town is far from an ideal site for solar construction, but the land had been bought and the utility work had been done on it before the solar idea firmly took hold. Not surprisingly, given the vaulting terrain here, a large hill rises to the south and blocks the low winter sun by early afternoon. So how can solar heating work if the sun shines only half the time to begin with, and when it does shine, its rays hit the buildings for only part of the day?

Well, Cecil Turk will show you how. You walk upstairs to the "furnace" on the second story. It is a bare-bones solar-heating unit, basically an attic with plastic glazing instead of standard roofing, and it is designed for the sole purpose of capturing the warmth of the sun's rays and then transferring heat to the store below, if necessary. This solar furnace is upstairs, because putting it at that modest elevation means that the heater — with walls and floors painted black to absorb solar radiation more effectively — can run on the sun's flames for a little bit longer than if it were at ground level. Cecil's unconventional furnace added about $6,000 to the cost of his new store, but he figures he saved that much in fuel bills in the first few years. After the IGA had weathered its first three winters, Cecil had yet to set a match to the pilot light of the backup furnace.

The skeptics think little of this accomplishment because, as they are quick to point out, in heating the building, Cecil can take advantage of all the waste heat given off by the compressors that refrigerate the store's many coolers. And Cecil does take advantage of that waste heat. The true non-believers seem to think that by making this point, they have given the solar design of the new IGA a decisive knock. But supermarkets in nearby Viroqua or Richland Center have compressors that give off as much waste heat as Cecil's do, yet the designs of their buildings fail to take advantage of that gift. Instead, those stores rely on furnaces to keep shoppers warm through winter. As Tom Hirsch, former relocation coordinator and solar adherent, says, "I don't care if the sun doesn't shine one day. First and foremost, what that project is about is energy conservation." The view from Cecil Turk's IGA reveals that some things were clearly done right here.

A number of things were done wrong, too, if truth be told. The solar village is ugly. Everyone — and I mean everyone, not just artists and photographers, but also the town's residents — admits it. Even the architect does.

Rodney Wright was working as an architect in Chicago when he took on the Soldiers Grove project. He did preliminary studies and overall site planning and he designed a number of the buildings, including Cecil Turk's. To do the job, he moved to his vacation home in Osseo, Wisconsin, about two hours north of town, and commuted almost daily.

Although an elfin man with a genial round face and white beard, Wright gives emphasis to his speech with regular, if mild, profanity. There is a friendly gruffness to his tone. Of course the buildings in town look cheap and are ugly, he says. "Hell, the town didn't have any damn money. That's what's tragic about the whole thing." The buildings are sided in textured plywood that apes vertical boards, and they are painted various earth tones — muddy, ocherous hues. (One prospering owner of a solar-heated store asked, "Do they look like chicken coops to you? We had a coop at home that looked like this — only it was white.")

The landscaping around the buildings was never completed. Lacking trees and shrubs, the new village still, several years after all hammering and sawing had been finished, has the look of a recent construction site. Originally, Wright had proposed building a covered walkway to link the shops and offices in the village. Aesthetically it would have tied the buildings together, and practically it would have provided some protection in winter. A number of people disliked the idea of the walkway, though, and it was never built. And as a result, the town looks like a work in progress.

Looking back, Wright says that the people of Soldiers Grove were "nuts" to have attempted the relocation project. He means it as a compliment. Even today, thinking about what the people accomplished under pressure and with little money, Wright almost visibly sags under the weight of it: "The effort, man. Jesus."

Under the best conditions, architect-client relations are delicate, and they often become strained — and that happens when the client *wants* to build a new house. In Soldiers Grove, Wright was not hired by a single willing client, but instead he in effect worked for hundreds, or at least scores, of clients, and to a certain extent they were being forced into new buildings. Now that the work is done, it would take Diogenes' successor to find anyone who has a nice word to say about him. He was asked to do an impossible job, and I do not know whether he expected thanks for the job he did, but he will get none around here. The townspeople think he milked them.

And how lucrative was the project for Wright? "You mean other than losing my ass?" he replies. He says that he put in $20,000 to $30,000 worth of unbilled hours.

Despite the disaffection of Soldiers Grove with its architect, what finally matters most may be, as Wright declares, "at least the town is high and dry."

Happy hour at the Wonder Bar produces fewer smiles than you would hope to see. The bar is shaped something like a question mark, and most patrons are seated around the curve, where the taps and bottles are — the straight run is opposite the grill and deep fryer, a bit out of the action. On the wooded bar, patrons' hands encircle drafts of Pabst in glasses or Heileman's Old Style, a local favorite, in cans. Hurless Briggs favors brandy and seltzers. "It's a good thing they don't taste good. Otherwise I might really put them away." These days Hurless works up a thirst doing some painting — he lets a hired man work the small dairy farm that has been his for years. Hurless, like many of the customers at this hour, is closer to receiving a Social Security check than a draft card. He remembers when Soldiers Grove was a town to be proud of, when, for example, it had seven bars. "They used to call us Little Hurley," he says, explaining that the real thing is a town in the northern part of the state noted for fast — and loose — living.

The Wonder Bar is the only action in town now, but at the time of the flood, several others offered competition. That loss gripes people. Anyone who wants a drink does not appear to be having problems getting one, but they do miss the varied choices of old, the richer social possibilities.

Listening to the talk, you wonder if the Corps of Engineers might have been right about one thing, that relocation was "socially unacceptable." Patrons complain that when the town was moved, some businessmen simply took their disaster-relief money and called it a day. Others took that money plus additional relocation money, but then chose to set up shop elsewhere. As Cecil Turk says, "They got their relocation money and just picked up and left the county. They didn't help us hold our town together." There were thirty-nine businesses in the old town. There are fewer than half that number in the solar village. John Young, who owns a television store and gun shop, decorated with the racks of thirty-nine deer, admits, "I miss the old Main Street. You could go next door and have coffee with your neighbor." Now, the new restaurant stands empty; two different owners have been unable to make a go of it. You can get burgers and fries at the Wonder Bar, though. And during happy hour, along with half-price drinks, popcorn sits on the counter. People munch, swill, and complain.

John Young explains, "There are some that never will like the new town, but anytime you have a change, there's some of that element anyway."

A fellow shopkeeper in the new village adds, "Most of the grumblers are the ones who didn't have to worry about the water coming in the back door and taking the groceries out the front."

Despite the grumbling, people return. One of the striking phenomena of small-town America is that the young leave, but the old keep coming home. A former military man, unshaven now and surely a larger target than in his combat days, says, "I'm just like some smelly fish coming back to where it was spawned."

Don Stoebner has been in Soldiers Grove only a few years. An advertisement in *Drug Store News*, a trade journal, caught his eye — the town was looking for a pharmacist — so he signed on. He borrowed enough to buy the building next to Cecil Turk's IGA, borrowed some more for operating expenses, and went into business dispensing drugs.

In his late thirties, Stoebner is a chunky man of medium height. He wears black-rimmed glasses, and his pants bag down over the heels of his thick-soled black laced shoes. Born in North Dakota, he views himself as a fortunate man to have arrived in Soldiers Grove, which to his mind is right in the middle of the action. Minneapolis is only five hours to the northwest, Chicago a mere five hours to the southeast. Milwaukee is closer. When you come from the northern expanses, you get used to driving long distances, and traveling a few hours to see a baseball game or hear the symphony is no big deal.

For someone from Grant County, North Dakota, with 2,500 square miles, three paved roads, and 4,500 people, adjusting to Wisconsin, with its denser population and its more numerous regulations, resulted in culture shock. But Don and Bonnie Stoebner also like the possibilities their new homestead offers. Back in Carson, no one could conceive of a self-sufficient little operation on just a few acres. Out on the prairies, the basic field is a section, 640 acres, one square mile. "Everything is neatly arranged in squares," Stoebner recalls. "Here the roads follow the contours, and a field is anywhere they can find a flat place." On their little 4½-acre homestead outside Soldiers Grove, the Stoebners, lifetime subscribers to *Mother Earth News,* are exploring all manner of possibilities — goats and gardens and orchards. They have tried tapping maple trees and making syrup, and they have hiked into the spring woods to hunt for prized morel mushrooms.

In North Dakota, they used to get tasty homegrown

chicken from the Hutterites, a communal farming sect. After eating storebought chicken in Soldiers Grove, they decided to raise their own. They fed 200 birds, and, come slaughtering time, "We butchered until the freezer was full and bought another freezer," according to Bonnie Stoebner. The Stoebners filled the second freezer and still had six birds left over, so they bartered them for cider. Now when chicken is served, the kids do not complain that the meat tastes like cardboard.

Their boy, Joseph, is almost a teenager, with a suitably hip rattail trickling down the back of his neck. "We voted no to an earring," Bonnie remarks. Their daughter, unlike themselves, finds Soldiers Grove too isolated. "Her whole personality is geared for constant action," Bonnie says, so that child attends high school in cosmopolitan Prairie du Chien (pronounced "prayer do sheen"), and boards with a family in that Mississippi River town forty miles away.

Don and Bonnie are making an effort to take advantage of their new hometown. Bonnie — who served in the military — is a member of the American Legion, and Don bowls with the team. Bonnie also helps head up 4-H activities locally. "We don't stay at home; we get involved," Don says, and Bonnie chimes in, "Whether they want us or not." Every Thursday, they drive up to Viroqua for tae kwon do class (along with Dr. John, the new dentist, the town's first in thirty years). The teacher/master is Korean, leading Bonnie to comment: "It's amazing the people hidden in the hills."

You hear talk about how bad business is in town, but the pharmacy is doing OK, and the Stoebners, perhaps inspired by their experimentation on the homestead, are trying new commercial ventures also. For example, they are putting money into videocassette rentals. And even if the tape is peeling off the wallboard in the solar attic, they have to pay only $500 to $600 a year for heat.

"We like it here," Bonnie says, "even if we are nerds."

"Bullet" Bob Peterson is unusual in many regards, not the least of which is that he is a rare combination: both a native of the town and an admirer of the state's Department of Natural Resources, which is an agency often cited by people here for sticking its nose where they think it does not belong. But, as Peterson says, "One of the best things about this state is its clean air and clean water. You have to protect that." Also, in this "community that never mixed well," as one resident said of Soldiers Grove, Peterson is one of the natives who did develop bonds with those who moved here.

Peterson was a fine athlete as a boy, and his speed earned him his nickname — which turns out to have been a grim bit of foreshadowing. Unlike the old soldier at the Wonder Bar, Peterson would never call himself a smelly fish, but he, too, is a military man who came home — in a wheelchair after a Vietnamese bullet found his spine. Although he is president of the village trustees, he is not nearly as busy as he was when the relocation was underway. He spends much of his time at home, an earth-bermed house designed by Tom Hirsch, the departed relocation coordinator, located across the river and over the hill from the solar village. Animated in conversation, he quickly shifts to self-consciousness when the talk lags.

In a way, his recent life has somewhat paralleled the village's. The energy and expectations of the solar village have given way to the grinding realities of everyday limitations.

Being the nation's first solar town brought Soldiers Grove some publicity and a flush of optimism, but it has not brought prosperity. A few new businesses have set up in town — the pharmacy and a nursing home — but there are fifteen empty lots in the solar village. Furthermore, a solar village has not changed the nature of the farm economy hereabouts, where the signs on the road advise: "Every month is dairy month."

"The so-called good times never trickled down this far," Bob says. The solar village has physically lifted the town, but no one's spirits are terribly elevated these days, Bob's included: "This didn't make people pull together the ways we were hoping they would."

One person who lives a dozen miles outside of town described the old Soldiers Grove as something of a "roughneck town." Lots of people were comfortable with that and the bars. Now they have this new unfamiliar town, and they look back fondly. Bob Peterson would not mind having back the difficult but forward-looking days after the big flood, the days that brought hope and new arrivals, imaginative people like Tom Hirsch. "They were outstanding people," he says. "They helped us a lot."

As another resident said, "The new solar town couldn't have been done by the newcomers alone, but it couldn't have been done without them." Probably no one would disagree, but, ultimately and unhappily, it seems a solar village is not Soldiers Grove's image of itself. It seems that for towns as for many people, hanging onto an old and familiar persona — no matter how flawed — feels more comfortable than daring to take the risk of a new approach.

Floods used to be bad medicine in Soldiers Grove, but today a torrent would be tonic. The town has not had much more than mud puddles since the deluge of 1978. As a result, everyone seems to have forgotten the mess high water can make.

This "floodplain amnesia," as one commentator called it, is similar to the forgetfulness that afflicts all of us about past trials, unpleasantness, and pain. The living-room furniture floating in the bedroom, the wainscoting of mud, the lost heirlooms and small private treasures, the daunting costs — these memories fade.

A flood would provide the necessary reminder, but without any accompanying damage and dislocation, that relocation was bold and wise. Soldiers Grove is floodproofed and basking in the sun. That is the wonder of this town, and its source of sadness too.

Pray for rain.

Chapter 10

THE LAKE THAT NEVER WAS

OSCEOLA, MISSOURI — "Welcome to Came-
lot," the sign says in black paint, clumsily hand-
lettered. A gravel drive leads off Highway B just
north of town and runs under a power line. It
heads past a stiff, tiger-striped cat with a pool of
blood dried below its throat and proceeds along the edge of
an immature oak woods. Pole-sized oaks have been bulldozed into piles beside the driveway, and numbered stakes
with surveyor's tape mark out lots, from one to three acres.
The asking price is $2,000 per acre. Camelot is for sale.

But no one is buying. Osceola is a town with a past. Its
future is muddy.

"Where the Ozarks Meet the Plains," says the sign along
the highway at Lowry City, six miles north of Osceola. "We
kinda feel they stole that from us," says Lois Belisle, the
Osceola town clerk. It is a sentiment that her fellow townspeople share. The sign is, in fact, out of place at Lowry City,
sitting as it does where the land has flattened out beyond
the Ozark foothills. It belongs in Osceola, where the plains
and the mountains literally flow together.

The town sits on the southern shore of the Osage River, just downstream from the Osage's confluence with the Sac. Sediment-laden tributaries of the Osage drain southeastern Kansas and come together to form the Osage in western Missouri. To the south, the Sac spills out of the gravel streambeds of the Ozarks. Prairie drainage and mountain river join at Osceola.

Historically, this was also a meeting ground — a battleground, actually — of two cultures. In the years prior to the Civil War, abolitionist and proslavery raiders terrorized southwestern Missouri and southeastern Kansas. Kansas Jayhawkers, including the notorious John Brown, fought to keep Kansas a free state. In return, Bushwhackers, Missouri's guerrillas, fought to push slavery into Kansas. In 1861, General Jim Lane of Lawrence, Kansas, raided Osceola, plundering the town and burning it to the ground.

Two years later, Missourians got revenge. William Quantrill led a band of guerrillas into Lawrence, killing some 150 men and boys. General Lane escaped, hiding in a corn field. Riding with Quantrill were several Missourians who would go on to achieve fame — or infamy — after the war: Frank James, brother of Jesse, was one. Also along for the sport were a few of the Younger brothers, whose father had been killed by Jayhawkers and who would later ride with the James gang. One admiring biographer of Jesse James, writing in the 1880s, said of Missouri's Bushwhackers, "Fiercer than Bedouin Arabs, confident as the Mamelukes, they united the infinite physical endurance of the Western Indian and the indomitable soul and mental qualities of the Anglo-Norman."

After the war, the Jameses and Youngers embraced crime, although their supporters would say that, as unrepentant Southern patriots, they were forced to live outside the bounds of society. In robbing banks and railroads controlled by their Northern conquerors, they were viewed as Robin Hood's New World heirs.

Although not native to Saint Clair County, where Osceola is the county seat, the Youngers had many friends here and regularly hid out in a cave just upstream at Monegaw Springs. In 1874, John Younger was killed by a Pinkerton detective hired by one of the Youngers' irate corporate victims. John Younger died in nearby Roscoe, where today the Confederate flag still flies alongside the Stars and Stripes at the log office of the Osage Mercantile, which will serve you breakfast and sell you a loaf of bread and a fishing license.

Osceola was a thriving town at the start of the Civil War. Steamboats sailed up from the Missouri River all the way to town. When war broke out, the population was 2,077. When peace came, the population was 183. Today it sits at 841.

"Lake View Estates," says the sign, whose words cannot deceive the eye.

Osceola had fixed its hopes for civic rejuvenation on Truman Lake, an impoundment that was created when the U.S. Army Corps of Engineers dammed the Osage sixty-two meandering, riverine miles downstream at Warsaw in 1979.

"A lot of people was really pumped up," says Tip Coleman, proprietor of the Osage Mercantile. "They expected sand beaches, waterskiing, wide vistas."

But "lake" is not the term to describe the view at Osceola. "Mud flats" is. Snags protrude from the shallows;

driftwood and debris are washed up on the flats. The current of the Osage slows, and Kansas sediment fills the channel and coves around town. "We're just a backwater," says a dispirited Osceola storeowner, his secondhand goods laid out on tables.

Truman Dam at Warsaw holds back the water not only of the Osage (and its Kansas tributaries) but also of Tebo Creek, the South Grand River, and the Pomme de Terre (pronounced locally as "pommity tar"), creating a gnarled, four-fingered lake with a surface area of 55,600 acres. That is the size of the so-called multipurpose pool, or power pool, the size of the lake as masterminded by the Corps of Engineers. Its surface sits, as planned, at 706 feet above sea level. All it would take to put a smile on Osceola would be to raise the level of the lake eight or nine feet, thereby covering the snags and mud flats with fresh water as clear and blue as a sunny midwestern sky.

Truman Dam could easily accommodate such a rise in the water level. The higher level would cause the heavy siltation to occur well upstream of Osceola, enabling the town to build a marina and thereby promote recreation locally. It would mean, in the modest assessment of one townsman, "We'd have the best fishing in the YOU-nited States."

As a result, when discussing their plight, Osceolans often begin sentences with "If the Corps would only raise the lake to 715 . . ." It is a fascinating sentence, rising up out of determined ignorance or, more often, an inability to accept that the worst has happened and will not be undone. It expresses a belief so fundamental to human nature: that our problems would be solved if only someone else would mend his ways. But Osceola, like a forlorn individual, is stuck with what it is stuck with.

For starters, the corps is not about to raise the water level of Truman Lake, spending additional tens of millions to undermine a $550 million project, just to mollify a town of 841 disappointed people. Truman Dam is a flood-control dam, among other things. (It also generates power, far less than originally planned, a sore point among Osceolans.) If the lake were filled to the 715-foot level, the corps would have to buy up thousands of acres of land (at an estimated cost of $30 million), which the lake's waters would then permanently cover. Currently it has only acquired flowage easements on that land, allowing water to inundate it temporarily during flooding. A 715-foot water level would also eliminate some 20 percent of Truman Dam's flood-controlling capacity. A 715-foot level would eliminate siltation in the water around Osceola, but "we'd just force our trouble on somebody else upstream," admits Dick Kiefer, a real estate agent whose office is on the town square.

As a rule, people in Osceola are unimpressed with Truman Dam's performance during high water. That is because they are on the wrong side of the dam. When it rains in Kansas, they get soggy in Osceola.

Those downstream of the dam stay dry, however, as planned.

"When the people of Osceola heard 'flood control,' they thought it meant flood control here," says Beth Cox, whose few-times-great-grandfather was a Confederate senator from Osceola. By holding back floodwaters for downstream communities, Truman Dam has caused major fluctuations in water levels upstream around Osceola. The temporary rise in water has not exceeded the bounds prescribed by the corps when it bought flowage easements, but the fluctuations have been more frequent and more severe than Osceolans had anticipated.

As a result, people around town say, "The old floods were never like this. It never got nearly so high as it did last year."

They say, with an unintended pun, "The corps' calculations weren't worth a damn. This is one of the poorest surveyed pools of water in the whole country."

They say, "We've had three hundred-year floods since they put the dam in."

One local analyst neatly, if blasphemously, summed up the Osceolan view. "The corps says the flooding's an act of God, but God didn't do anything until the corps came along."

According to weather records compiled by the corps since Truman Dam became operational, the Osage River basin has been unnaturally wet. Between 1982 and 1987, the average flow of water into the basin has been at least 30 percent higher than the annual average for the previous forty-five years. Even so, none of the so-called hundred-year floods has actually reached the hypothetical hundred-year benchmark, although rising water got close in October 1986. Within a four-week span, twenty-eight inches of rain fell in parts of the Truman basin; the corps estimates that a full year's worth of water flowed into the lake during that one-month span. Eventually the water level reached 738.74 feet above sea level. The top of the flood pool is 739.6 feet.

"Flood control worked beautifully," Everett L. Bell, resource manager with the corps, says. The corps estimates that in the fall of 1986, Truman Dam prevented some $200 million in flood damages. "The water would have overtopped Bagnall Dam," which was built by a private power company in 1929 and backs up water for the better-known, splashier Lake of the Ozarks, the resort of choice.

"I think you just said a bad word," Lois Belisle remarks, at city hall. Lake of the Ozarks is a highly developed resort lake on which many of the state's business and political leaders own valuable property. In addition, Bagnall Dam, unlike Truman Dam, is privately owned and not designed for flood control. What Osceolans have concluded, to their annoyance and at some cost to their self-esteem, is that their town is being sacrificed to protect powerful private interests elsewhere.

"We know we're flood control for Lake of the Ozarks," says J. D. Booker, president of the Osceola Chamber of Commerce.

Dick Kiefer adds, "This dam is about a clear lake at Lake of the Ozarks. We're just a big settlement pool for them."

Booker says, "It's politics, a power struggle."

It may, indeed, be politics, be about power, but it appears not to be a struggle. There never was much of one, and what struggle there was, was no contest.

"Lake Shore Estates," says the sign. Not true. There are no estates, no tiny cottages even, on the shore. From the developer's viewpoint, the shoreline of Truman Lake is purely, untouchably virgin. It remains safely in the chaste hands of the corps, which acquired 165,679 acres to be covered by the impoundment. None of the publicly held land may be used for private enrichment.

In Osceola, the frustration of failing to see prosperity

result from the creation of the lake is compounded by the loss of taxable property that has become lake bottom. One quarter of Osceola's tax base sank under Truman's waters.

"It ruined the damn county," says Frank Kottwitz, chewing manfully on the soggy end of an unlit cigar. Old enough no longer to be bound by convention, although I doubt he ever felt so restricted, Kottwitz speaks freely in a gravelly voice: "I always had a habit of mouthin' off," he says. "This was a farming community, but they keep thinking they're going to have something," as though something — anything — would be better to have than farming. Kottwitz is a farmer and runs a fertilizer business on the side.

The lake has been unkind to the farmers. "The corps took all of our good ground — your bottom land in this part of the country is your best ground. You could make hundred-bushel corn on it."

Now it is underwater, and what isn't submerged still gets planted — but at some risk to the farmer. If the fall rains are heavy, as they have been, come harvest time the impoundment controls the high water and protects second-home owners on the shoreline of Lake of the Ozarks — "the money people," Kottwitz calls them — by backing up water onto the corn ground.

Frank Kottwitz is pissed off, and he's glad to tell you. "They ruined our economy."

"St. Clair County Hilton," says the sign in front of the one-story brick building under construction next to the town square. "Hilton" is written on a piece of cardboard attached to the sign; underneath it says, "Jail."

"It's a monstrosity of a damn deal they're building,"

Kottwitz complains. "The county don't have the money to operate it."

The county cannot, in fact, afford to run the new jail, which the corps is building because the old jail sits on the flood plain. The sheriff, Fred M. Haworth, Jr., is, however, undeterred. He sees opportunity where others see folly. As the cardboard of the sign suggests, he plans to rent out rooms — to overcrowded federal and state prisons. "The federal government is hard pressed finding places for its prisoners. I think with leasing out the extra beds, the jail will pay for itself," Haworth says.

Because the new jail is being built with federal money, it will have to meet all current Justice Department standards for correctional facilities, and it will have to be run according to federal guidelines. Haworth believes the sheriff's department will need a minimum of ten people to run the new jail. That's quite a change for a department that has the equivalent of two full-time paid staff, in addition to Haworth: a deputy, a three-quarters-time deputy, and a part-time dispatcher. In 1986 the department had the equivalent of three and a half deputies. "The next year was a bad year," Haworth comments. "The county commissioners balanced the budget. Unfortunately it cost us the sheriff's department. By all rights we should have shut the jail down." To help out with local law enforcement, a number of people in town pitched in as volunteers, working as dispatchers and reserve officers. "I can't think of anywhere else in county government where people are donating their time," Haworth says. Wearing leather slippers on a Saturday morning, he is sitting in the cramped office of the old jail, three desks jammed into a room that might be all of twelve feet by sixteen.

A former Kansas City policeman, Haworth moved to Saint Clair County in 1972 "to get away from drugs" while he raised a family. Before the new jail opened, he was running the sheriff's office on a budget of $64,000. "It's almost a disgrace," he says, then adds, "It ain't almost — it is a disgrace."

Since being voted into office in 1984, Haworth has become adept at scrounging. He persuaded a government agency to donate patrol cars — with 80,000 to 100,000 miles on them — and he cajoles spare parts out of a friend who runs a cab company.

"Nineteen eighty-seven was just survival." In 1986, Haworth estimated the street value of marijuana confiscated in drug busts in the county to be $3.5 million. "This southern Missouri is known for pot, anymore," he says. "We teach a lot of our kids in agriculture school very good," he adds, a big smile appearing as he offers this wry estimate of local education. In 1987, with the force depleted of personnel, the street value of marijuana confiscated was a mere $0.5 million. "Half a million's a laugh," he says ruefully.

Haworth introduces Black Jack: "This is my marijuana dog." A few days earlier, the black Labrador sniffed out the stash of one of the prisoners in the county jail. To demonstrate Black Jack's talents, Haworth unlocks a file cabinet and pulls out a Baggie of dope. He holds it toward Black Jack and calls him. The dog doesn't move or make a sound. Haworth tries again. Nothing. Black Jack remains mute and rooted, no more interested in Haworth's lure than a fat trout in a plastic worm. Haworth shrugs, puts the dope away, and sends Black Jack down to the cellar.

The new jail will bring in about $150,000 in revenue a year, according to Haworth. In the first couple of years, he expects hiring and training of staff and general operating costs to eat up the income. Eventually, though, Haworth calculates the jail could make money for the county, and early indications are that Haworth's estimates were on target.

The sheriff has heard the grumbling about importing criminals from outside the community; he understands there is some bite in the designation of the new jail as the "Hilton." He responds by saying, "Even when some people are handed a gold brick, they complain because it is too heavy. Ten jobs in this area would mean quite a lot."

"Small Engine Sirvice. Boat Motoers. Lawnmowers," the sign says. No matter how you spell the jobs, work is difficult to find. Fred Haworth's children are up in Kansas City, 125 miles to the north, raising their families. "They would like to be back down here," Haworth says, "but there is no work down here."

Beth Cox's husband has a job in Kansas City and spends weekends with the family in Osceola, a not uncommon approach. Others manage by working in Kansas City for brief spells. A union electrician says he can earn $17 an hour in the city, but only $6 an hour, "if you're lucky," in Osceola — assuming you can find the work in the first place.

So what do people do?

"What would you think about welfare?" one storekeeper asks.

"The women work, but the men don't," an outspoken young woman explains. "Then the wives come home and cook supper, and the men tell them how to vote."

There is Social Security, which helps prop up the many

older people who live in town, having returned to a family place after years away.

Or military pensions, which support people like an air force veteran, Bob Whitehead, the mayor, who arrived in Osceola a few years ago. "Really, you can't count too much on making a living in this area," he says.

"RV Hotspot on Truman Lake," the sign at the edge of town says. It is a monument either to mankind's eternal optimism or the species' enduring capacity for self-deception. The fishing is good, everyone agrees, especially for catfish, and they figure there just has got to be a way to translate that into prosperity. Except, as Dick Kiefer says, "generally the kind of people who go after catfish aren't the kind who spend a lot of money."

"That's what pisses me off," Frank Kottwitz says. "Recreation is all right, but — " and then only profanity, vigorously aired, can express his disgust. Of the people who speed past town on Highway 13, headed who knows where, intending to spend as little as possible, he says, "They got a damn camper hooked behind their damn four-wheel-drive pickup and they got a damn twelve-thousand-dollar boat behind their damn camper and they got a damn rack on the front of their damn pickup with a pair of damn dirt bikes on it." Case closed.

Osceola used to be the spoonbill capital of the United States. A spoonbill, or paddlefish, *Polydon spathula*, is a spatula-snouted curiosity that grows to five feet in length and weighs sixty pounds. It is a primitive fish, with a skeleton of cartilage rather than bone. Its sole relative is a rare fish in China. It used to breed in a fifty-five-mile stretch of gravel-bottomed river between Osceola and the dam site in Warsaw, but siltation that has resulted from the impoundment of the Osage's sediment-rich water has buried the gravel beds preferred by spoonbills. According to Kim Graham, a paddlefish biologist with the Missouri Department of Conservation, "We lost ninety-nine-point-nine percent of our spoonbill breeding with Truman Dam." There are only a few remnant breeding spoonbill populations elsewhere in the Missouri River drainage.

Come spring in the old days, fishermen would flock to Osceola, intent on landing the large, preposterous fish resembling some mythological hybrid — perhaps Zeus, having so enjoyed disporting as a swan, decided to return as a deep-diving duck and mischievously take his pleasure with a swordfish. Fisherman would line the river banks and stand shoulder to shoulder along the small dam that used to block the river here. The fish were not lured with bait, but rather were snagged blindly with large treble hooks dragged through the water. An ignoble business, that jigging, but many of our sports, whether they are between man and man or man and creature, have a cruel streak. Today, because of the lost breeding grounds, spoonbill fishing is prohibited on the lake — and if it is ever allowed again, the paddlefish expert Kim Graham admits, "Any spoonbill fishery will be maintained by hatchery-raised fish."

Truman Lake was going to make the old spoonbill fishing days seem like small fry. Now everyone in town would weep thankfully at their return.

Outside Osceola, though, there seems small concern for its diminished state. The truth is that no matter what the basic water level of the lake, some people someplace would have to put up with siltation and, in a rainy season, flooding. As Dale Gronewald, the project manager of Truman Dam and Lake, says flatly of Osceola's plight, "The lake has to have an upper end somewhere."

To which Mayor Bob Whitehead responds: "The corps' comment now is 'Everyone knows the upper portions of a reservoir is no good.' I didn't hear that until 1987. That's why people are pretty perturbed."

"Troublemakers and Anyone Fighting Will Be Barred!!" says the sign on the door of the Steak House, a roadhouse just north of town on Highway 13.

"We used to have a lot of tavern fights, but not anymore," Sheriff Haworth says. Still, this can be violent country, and the sign is a reminder to those who might grow forgetful of their manners late in the evening. Such an occurrence would come as no surprise to anyone, long-time customer or first-time onlooker.

Patrons sport cowboy boots, sleeveless T-shirts, earrings, tattoos. Male and female alike curse loudly. A game of pool is underway, while couples dance to Andy Johnson, "the best picker around." Johnson, a husky man with a bent toward singing the blues, has played behind Kate Taylor, James Taylor's sister, and Linda Ronstadt. In his late thirties now and a family man, he has returned to the ancestral home in Osceola, where he drives a school bus and on weekends picks expertly.

Away from the dance floor, one good old boy, dressed in coveralls and wearing a weathered cowboy hat, holds court at a large table. His blood fired with canned spirits, he details his conquest of a young lady from Pittsburgh. One can imagine he would employ the same delivery to recount his landing of a record paddlefish. With his story complete, and apparently having inspired himself by his own account of his youthful panache, he gets up. "It's time to go," he says, "but before I do, I think I'll find me a woman without any stretch marks to dance with."

"Rural Missouri Cooking At Its Best," says the sign outside the restaurant of the Old Plantation Motel. Down here, that means barbecue — ribs, beef, pork, and ham — catfish, and biscuits and gravy, this latter a breakfast favorite that looks like wallpaper paste and must surely be a cruelty on the cardiovascular works.

But the happy truth is, people do not seem to be worrying themselves on that score. Despite their complaints, despite being at the wrong end of the lake and the lack of economic prospects, Osceolans seem happy enough to be where they are.

"This is the most beautiful part of the state," Bob Whitehead says.

"It's easy livin'," says Barney Barnes, who owns the real estate office in which Whitehead works.

"Fisherman, hunters, they like our area," Dick Kiefer says.

"I can let my children run up and down the sidewalk and I don't have to worry about their being taken. We leave the keys in our car, our house open," Beth Cox says.

Their town is uncorrupted by celebrity, which is perhaps not what they had wished for, but may be the better state. It is true, almost everyone has to scramble to make ends meet, but they are scrambling in a place where they are happy to be. Perhaps someday, when New England and

northern California have been divided and further subdi-
vided into odd lots and remainders and when the popular
lake-shore counties of the upper Midwest have been overrun, Osceola will have its day. People will buy up Camelot — and it will be Camelot no more.

Chapter 11

HARD-ROCK MINERS AND THE COWBOY BLUES

NYE, MONTANA — Jan Myers grew up outside Boston and married a sailor from out West. "After he got out of the service, he said he was going to take me to Montana," recalls Jan, who was a teenager at the time. "I didn't dare ask him what a Montana was."

Lou Myers remembers that they landed back in Big Timber, to the north of Nye. He hooked up with a man who was breaking horses in the livestock corrals by the railroad yards. "We had elk steaks for breakfast," Lou recounts, "as much beer as you could drink, and pens full of green stock. One day Jan asked me, 'When are you going to get a job?'

" 'This is it,' I told her. We had it made."

For a time anyway. Since then, Lou has led Jan, who had, in his words, "a stay-put childhood," on a tour of the modern American West. "He once asked me why I always stayed near him when we first got married," Jan says. "That was because most of the time, I didn't know where I was."

They leased a ranch in the Dakota Badlands until they got "drouthed out." Lou guided hunters into the mountains north of Yellowstone Park, and he logged near Bridger, Montana. For the past seventeen years, he has been a hard-rock miner, "tramping around." He dug uranium in Jeffrey City, Wyoming, copper and nickel in Montrose, Colorado, tungsten in Winnemucca, Nevada, and silver in Kellogg, Idaho. When the price of silver fell and the future of the Sunshine Mine, where he was working, looked doubtful, Lou took aim on Nye. "I tramped out and headed over here," where a new mine was about to make the transition from exploration to production. Soon he was promoted to shift boss for the Stillwater Mining Company, which in the spring of 1987 opened up the only platinum mine in the United States.

More than 92 percent of the world's platinum supply (3.2 million ounces) comes from two countries, South Africa and the Soviet Union, with South Africa being by far the largest supplier. Modest amounts of platinum are used by the electronics, chemical, and glass industries, but plati-num's major role is in automobiles. Platinum is relatively inert chemically; it takes extraordinary temperatures to melt it, and its surface properties are such that other elements combine at lower temperatures in its presence than they would otherwise. In sum, it is the ideal catalyst, an element that spurs a chemical reaction without entering into the re-action itself. Platinum is what makes the catalytic converter in your car work.

Despite its value — or perhaps because of it — this ele-ment is not reserved only for applications designed to better the world. In 1988, more than 25 percent of the world's platinum went to Japan to make jewelry, so many baubles that Japanese jewelers required more platinum (1.06 million ounces) than American automobile manufacturers did (690,000 ounces).

The demand for platinum continues to grow among European car makers as they equip more of their vehicles with emission controls (140,000 ounces were used in 1986, 305,000 ounces in 1988).

Experimentation with fuel cells, which convert chemical energy directly into electrical energy, suggests that platinum could in the future help to provide power to the electrical grid. Environmentally benign fuel cells, which use platinum electrodes, could be manufactured in relatively small units, say ten megawatts, making it possible for a utility to respond module-by-module to a growing call for electricity. Fuel cells are also attractive because they could be brought on-line more quickly than a typical three-hundred-megawatt coal- or oil-fired power plant. In addition to which, it has been said that a nation cannot wage a modern war without platinum.

Thus you have a "strategic metal" supplied by political outcasts on the one hand and political enemies on the other. It is a rare element used not only for sophisticated industrial and military purposes but also for luxury items. The result of such an uncertain and politically tainted supply yet unabating demand is that platinum has become a dandy investment. In 1982, 160,000 ounces worldwide were bought for speculative purposes; five years later, three times that amount was hoarded. In July of 1982, an ounce of platinum went for $286, and an ounce of gold went for $344. Seven years later, an ounce of platinum had climbed to $510, while an ounce of gold stood at $413.

Despite the platinum rush, the only place in the United

States where it can currently be found in quantities economical to mine is to the north of Yellowstone National Park, in the Beartooth Mountains overlooking the Stillwater River, about four miles south of Nye.

Holding down the clutter of papers on my desk at home is a heavy, coarse-grained rock. Its white and gray crystals, which are visible to the naked eye, had their genesis in the earth's fires 2.7 billion years ago, give or take a decade. If you tilt the rock slightly under the light, you can see sparkling yellow-green flecks. That's what the excitement here in Montana is all about. They are sulfides, in which can be found the platinum, about one ounce of it in every six tons of high-grade, ore-bearing rock. (About 3½ times as much palladium, a less valuable "platinum-group metal," is also present in the ore.)

Dick Vian, formerly a professor and now chief geologist at the Stillwater Mine, is explaining to me the fundamental geology of the platinum lode. He brings to my attention an article in a trade journal that he thinks will be helpful. It has sentences like "The Lower Banded Series comprises two repetitive gabbro to norite, troctolite and anorthosite cycles." And, "Sulfide minerals are net-textured throughout the matrix and also occur as fine disseminated grains to coarse interstitial clots." Vian views me as a marginal student, but there is enough residue of schoolmaster in him that he proceeds patiently, hoping perhaps that some personal attention may help the light enter my geologically benighted mind.

Vian's office is large and informal, with computer charts of geologic strata on the wall and a black metal bookcase holding volumes like *Geostatistical Ore Reserve Estimation*.

Holding a copy of *Geotimes* and pointing with a pen, he is demonstrating to me how the platinum came to be here. The igneous rock that contains it was laid down in a sheet, and, as the molten material cooled, it settled into distinct layers of different mineralogical composition. (A nearby vein of chromite was mined in the 1940s and 1950s, and copper and nickel deposits were found here back in the 1880s. "They thought they had found the largest nickel deposit in the world," Vian says. "There were some spectacular grades of ore, but they were not continuous.") Vian explains, "The rocks here are famous for this layered composition. Not many igneous rocks do that. People come from all over the world to see this."

About seventy million years ago, the layers were tilted, and here Vian demonstrates with his copy of *Geotimes*, turning up the unbound edge of the magazine. Instead of lying flat, the thin layer of platinum-bearing rock, called a reef, now angles upward into the mountain. Within this layer, the high-quality ore occurs in a wandering, broken seam that is as much as twenty feet wide in places, but elsewhere it narrows to nothing. Nobody knows how far down toward the core of the earth the reef extends. It runs twenty-eight miles from the eastern side of the Stillwater River west to the Boulder River.

The Stillwater Mining Company is a partnership of Johns-Manville, LAC Minerals, a Canadian mining concern, and Chevron, whose personnel actually run the operation. They have rights to six miles of the reef. On the basis of test drilling, Vian estimates that there will be enough good ore along that length to keep miners busy for thirty years.

The nature of the ore-bearing reef is such that it does not lend itself to bulk-mining techniques, in which great mechanical scoops remove pretty much all the rock. The high-grade ore must be tracked carefully by geologists to prevent "dilution." Company geologists take core samples every fifty feet to keep waste rock from bastardizing the ore, which would add considerably to the operation's mining and processing costs. "This ore is funny stuff to chase. It can be elusive," Lou Myers says. "At first, it was a tough puppy."

To get to the ore, the miners have blasted tunnels, called adits, into the side of the mountain about a hundred feet to the side of the reef. Then they blasted lateral tunnels over to the reef. They mine the ore from the bottom upward in vertical sections called stopes. Two-man teams work each stope. The stopes can be as narrow as three feet in some places. Dressed in coveralls, wearing hard hats, their feet protected by rubber boots into which are built brawny toe-and-metatarsal protectors of steel, the miners jackhammer and dynamite. Then they haul the rock out of the stopes using "slushers," buckets driven by small motorized winches. "Mining is awful hard on your body," a geologist, Jerry Doherty, comments.

It is dark in the mine, the only illumination coming from the miners' lamps and the lights of low-slung machinery that rumbles in and out, carrying ore. It is wet underground, with water running along the sides of the bedrock roadway. It is cool in the mine, a relief, some allege, from heat in the summer and cold in the winter.

"Anytime you're underground, it's dangerous," Dick Vian notes. To which Lou Myers comments: "This is probably the cleanest, safest mine in the United States." Lou is a big man, over six feet, rugged-looking and handsome, with a full mustache and impressive sideburns. He wears his miner's helmet cocked slightly down to the left, giving him a jaunty look. But mining is not a cavalier undertaking. "I've worked in some of the worst holes there is," Lou says. Down in the Sunshine Mine in Kellogg, five thousand feet below sea level, the temperature was 100°. "At the end of the day, you could pour the sweat out of your boot," Lou says. Having bored almost a mile toward the earth's molten core, "You were down there with the devil himself."

Dynamite and falling rock make hard-rock mining a risky occupation. As Lou Myers comments without pleasure, "I've packed a lot of guys out." Now he is working with men he may not have seen for a dozen years, experienced silver miners from Idaho and uranium miners from Utah who had been laid off and have converged on a new opportunity. "Refugees," one writer called them. "Top hands," Lou says. "We got a heckuva team, and we're trying to build a mine."

Lou and his fellows are taking out more than 700 tons of ore a day in two shifts. The mill that processes the ore operates seven days a week. In it, great rotating drums pulverize the ore; the resulting sand is run through a series of chemical baths to distill a concentrate that has approximately thirty-five ounces of platinum and palladium per ton. The platinumless crushed rock is returned to the mine, and the bags of concentrate are shipped to Belgium for smelting. At current production levels, the mine meets less than 5 percent of the United States demand for platinum — more than 10 percent for palladium — output that hardly protects the Free World from dependence on communist Russia or racist South Africa.

Having spent $60 million for mine exploration and development, the Stillwater group is pushing to get production up to 1,000 tons of ore per day, and they have budgeted the construction of a smelter on site, which would free the partners from the need to send the ore concentrate off to Belgium for refining. It does, after all, seem peculiar to send a ton of sand first across the continent and then across the Atlantic to end up with less than half a pound of platinum and a pound and a half of palladium. But construction of the smelter is no sure thing, for the mining operation has provoked opposition locally.

Noel Keogh, a young rancher whose place sits on the Stillwater River a few miles downstream from the mine, says, "It's no secret I'm no friend of the mine. I've got a lot at risk."

Joe Dewey, the Stillwater Mine project manager, admits to having gotten impatient with the requirements imposed on the mine by environmental regulations. He thinks the mine cannot be faulted for what it has done. For example, the consortium has built a tailings pond that covers thirty-nine acres, lined it with 100-mil plastic, and then surrounded it with $75,000 worth of chain link fence to keep out wildlife, especially local bighorn sheep, which could drown in the pond or puncture the lining. These steps have been taken so that none of the water used in mining and milling finds its way into the river. Given the fierce chemistry of the milling, the acid baths required to extract the platinum, the capture of this water from mining operations is no incidental concern to Keogh, whose livelihood would be directly threatened by its escape, and to others, who simply love this bony mountain country.

The mine is creating economic opportunities in the county, just as other mining ventures here have before. It has created jobs and paid taxes and impact fees. The ranchers acknowledge this. This is the Rocky Mountain West, after all, a vast, faulted terrain whose economy has always depended to a substantial degree on the extraction of its natural resources, especially timber, soft coal, and hard, fancy rocks. It is a land in which booms bring prosperity and brawling crowds, and busts empty out the towns and leave only the long-simmering feuds. The ranchers know all about the booms and the busts, and some of them still own their ranches today because of work they found in the chromium mines years ago. But people in the ranching community have, not surprisingly, a somewhat proprietary attitude toward this country. Go back no more than a single generation or two, and their forebears homesteaded this land — built log cabins in which, accompanied only by a neighbor and the wind blowing through the chinks, they birthed their babies. The miners, the nomads of Primacord, have come and gone. The ranchers, herders on horseback, arrive to stay. In spring, when Noel Keogh brands his calves, Donohoes and Russells, original Nye families, are there to help.

Indeed, a branding is to cattle country what a barn raising is to the Amish: some forty people, including spectators and children, show up to pitch in with the young stock at Keogh's up-country corrals. They arrive on horseback and in pickups, some taking the dirt road that swings behind the mine before it follows a narrow, steep course into the high grassland where Keogh's stock grazes.

Under a big sky, the sun leathering the skin, women set up tables with coffee and pastries. One of the volunteers grabs a warm beer — someone forgot the ice — from the bed of a truck. "It's noon, isn't it?" he asks. More like 9 A.M. "Somewhere in the world, it's past noon," he says, popping open the can.

Then, for the better part of the morning, three ropers on horseback drag calves out of the pens to pairs of muggers, who hold down the animals. One positions him- (or her-) self astride the head, a second neutralizes the hindquarters, gripping one leg, pressing forward on the hamstring of the other with a boot. The calves are branded, squalling and shitting when the hot steel singes their flank; vaccinated; dehorned, writhing as the buds are dug out of their skulls with a keen-edged tube; tagged, and, if necessary, castrated. This last procedure is one that inevitably causes some interior squirming among the men, who make light of it all. The calves lie quietly while Keogh slits their scrotums, grabs the two testicles, and pulls the spermatic cords out of the animals, slowly winding them around his hand. "That looks like it would hurt, don't it?" he remarks, and all nearby hands agree better the victim should be a drooling calf than some stout cowboy.

In the background, the cows bellow. The shaken young get to their feet, showing remarkable resilience, and scramble off to seek the solace of their dams.

The job is done shortly after noon, a couple of hundred head duly marked with a key and an O. The ground underfoot is pebbled with the horn buds; smears of green shit are everywhere, including on the muggers' pants. When I asked to come along to the branding, Keogh was concerned that I would treat it as an animal-rights issue. Raising cattle is an unsentimental business, and a rough one — on the cowboys, on the cows, and often on the range itself.

I'm not going to be cattle ranching's apologist. Neither am I going to beat up on the beef business. Ruminants are made so that they can turn grass, which is unpalatable to man, into meat, which is palatable to man. Their four legs enable them to chase the feed on ground too rough and steep to farm in other ways. There is good sense in this form of agriculture, if it is practiced sensibly. In the mountain West, grazing is often practiced on federal land leased to ranchers. Noel Keogh rents modest acreage, by western standards, from the government. In many places, the cattle have overgrazed western lands; streambanks have been trampled and the watercourses muddied. Native vegetation has given way to weeds; fish populations have suffered. Some people want the cattle off the government land — our land, not the cattlemen's — but do we have to drive the cattle off the land to remedy the problems? Uncompromising animal rightists and unbending environmentalists can have at Keogh and other cowboys — "swineherds on horseback," Edward Abbey called them — but what do we do with our western communities after we've chased the cows off the range? Do we care about a traditional working landscape, or do we want to turn all the ranchers into motel owners, changing the soiled linens of prosperous urbanites vacationing in the fresh mountain air?

For the moment, that prospect is distant, and the cattle are noisy in the background, calves smelling out mothers, mothers reciprocating.

With the day's work finished, the midday meal is served and the party is joined. Warm beer is no deterrent. A wildlife biologist for the state who had pitched in with the mugging talks up the reintroduction of wolves to the area. He asks the assembled cowboys, "Do you have any problems with

that?'' To which the reply is "No, I'd like to shoot a wolf.''
The crowd, warming to the occasion, then argues that the
grizzly bear should be taken off the endangered species list,
so the cowboys could shoot bears too. Arguments about
property rights ensue. The festivities, happily and disputa-
tiously underway, continue in one form or another until the
last poker pot is raked in at three the following morning,
and Noel Keogh has gotten the gamblers safely bedded
down in his basement. Along the way, the revelers play vol-
leyball and a rattlesnake gets itself killed and eaten. (Con-
trary to what you may have heard, rattlesnake does not taste
like chicken; it brings to mind anorexic fish.) A jug of something call R & R gets drunk. Events do not necessarily happen in that order.

By day's end, important work has been done and injuries
avoided, never a sure thing, given the wear and tear of cow-
boying. Everyone has enjoyed a celebration — the fabric of
the community shows itself as sturdy cloth. Ranching and
its rituals seem secure. For this one day, at least, no one
seems concerned about how a large — and perhaps expanding — mining operation might change life in the Stillwater
Valley.

"Obviously the mine has had an impact on the community,
as small as the community is," says Joe Dewey, who is always forthright. The mine is the largest employer in Stillwater County, and to help small communities cope with the
consequences of a new operation, Montana's hard-rock
mining law makes the mine responsible for the costs of additional government services created by the mine. For Stillwater Mining, that could be $2.5 million over three years

for sewers, roads, and bridges, the sheriff's office, welfare, the schools, and so on. "Everybody's on the shopping list," as Dewey puts it.

All of this money is not going to Nye itself, which isn't even a crossroads town. It is basically just a bar/restaurant/convenience store at a T where the dirt road heads off to follow the west branch of the Stillwater River. If you are not paying attention, you'll miss the sign

ENTERING AND LEAVING
NYE, MONTANA
ELEV. 4825 FT.

Just past the sign is a firehouse with two bays and grass growing in front of the doors. To the north are a log post office, with ninety boxes inside (and another ninety on the rural delivery route), and a credit union camped next door in a trailer. Nye has a cobblestone elementary school, but most of the children from the southern end of the county follow the river to Absarokee (pronounced "Absorkee"), twenty-five miles away, to go to school.

Mike Reynolds, the superintendent, says the mine added ninety students to the school, although about twenty-five have since left, creating a new transience in the community. "The mine did crowd us up," says Chuck Pfeil, a member of the school board, "but it didn't hurt our football team any."

"Yeah, we got about three horses," Reynolds says. He adds that the newcomers are more worldly than the natives of Absarokee. "They've taught our kids a few tricks," he says genially.

Space at school is nowhere near as limited as housing. Joe Dewey, the top man at the mine, is living in a trailer.

Many of the mining families are living near the mine in a mobile-home park put up by the company. Everything is fine in the mild weather, but come winter, the wind wails down the Stillwater Valley. Dick Vian says that the reading was 100 mph when a chinook blew the cups off the anemometer at the mine's weather station. Jan Myers remembers seeing some schoolchildren literally crawling toward the school-bus stop. "One little shooter was blown into the ditch." And a few trailers in the company park were rolled by the wind. Discussing the trailer park, Joe Dewey, as usual, does not mince words: "We missed the boat on that one."

After coming to Nye, Lou and Jan Myers lived for five months in a camper on company property. Eventually, they moved into an old ranch house without running water, and Lou dynamited the bedrock to put in a water line to a nearby spring. Jan got herself nine bum lambs to bottle-feed. They got a couple of horses and an Australian shepherd puppy named Poverty, which trails Lou, nipping at his heels. They are gradually fixing up the place and its 160 acres. Lou has spoken with Noel Keogh, who does spraying for the county, about having him come down the road and eradicate some weeds.

"I adapt," Lou says. "I make home wherever I wind up."

Jan is still close by. She has ascended into her forties, recently a grandmother. You would not know it to look at her. Her hair is black, her complexion flawless, her face unlined. She is a lovely woman, and it is difficult to imagine that she looks much older than she did when Lou first brought her to this strange land. Except now she knows where she is.

Chapter 12

TAKING ROOT

POINT REYES STATION, CALIFORNIA — Everyone here is from somewhere else. But this is California, so you knew that already. What is surprising is that even the ground under their feet is a new arrival, but, unlike the people, the ground is still on the move.

Point Reyes Station sits on the western edge of what geologists call the North American Plate. West of town is a peninsula of land that pushes out into the Pacific Ocean some twelve miles. The peninsula is part of the Pacific Plate. The meeting ground of these two plates, sixty-mile-thick bodies of the earth's crust, is the San Andreas Fault.

The Pacific Plate, whose granite bedrock matches that of southern California, is grinding northwest along the fault line at a rate of two inches per year, which means that in thirteen million years, more or less, Point Reyes Station will be a suburb of Los Angeles. The epicenter of the infamous 1906 earthquake was just a few miles south of Point Reyes Station at Dogtown, where, in the geological blink of an eye, the Pacific and North American plates snapped twenty feet past each other. In the 1989 quake, curiously, Point Reyes hardly felt a tremor.

Despite the unsettled state of the terra infirma and the certainty of further quakes to come, the residents of Point Reyes Station appear steady on their feet. It wasn't always that way. The latter-day settling of this town, both the arrival of newcomers and their maturing, in many ways exemplifies what has happened to a generation of rebels who are turning into adults all across the country. In that sense, this is a typical community.

It is an unusual place, too. Point Reyes Station sits at the foot of Tomales Bay in a valley between two ridges, pushed up by the pressure along the line of the San Andreas Fault. To the east are the hillside pastures of Bolinas Ridge. To the west is Inverness Ridge, forested with Douglas fir, bishop pine, and bay, and beyond Inverness Ridge is the northward-migrating peninsula. It runs about seventeen miles north of Point Reyes Station to the mouth of Tomales Bay and about fourteen miles south to the town of Bolinas. Viewed from the north, the peninsula looks a little like the leg of a field-goal kicker. Chimney Rock is his toe. The lighthouse sitting on the rocks of Point Reyes itself is the kicker's heel. The peninsula includes the Point Reyes National Seashore, 71,000 federally owned acres.

As one drops into town from the pastoral eastern approach, past modest one-story bungalows, a refurbished creamery appears on the right. Now given over to offices and studios, it houses Art Rogers, the "Town Photographer"; Mushroompeople, a mail-order supplier of spawn for shiitake mushrooms; Outdoor Adventures, a whitewater-rafting outfitter that guides trips down the Salmon, Tuolumne, and Lower Kern rivers, to mention a few; the Pulitzer prize-winning weekly newspaper, the *Point Reyes Light*. Across from the creamery, the Marin Agricultural Land

Trust, a nonprofit organization dedicated to preserving farmland in the county, shares quarters with the Farm Bureau,
an aging agricultural organization dedicated, it often appears, to stopping time. On the main north-south street, the
Palace Market has just been renovated, the roof having been
lifted to let in more natural light. Across the street, the Station House Café, a one-time hamburger joint, now serves
Philosopher's Salad and has been reviewed in *Gourmet*.

Despite the spiffy and exotic newcomers, it has been said
that this is still the kind of town where businesses are called
by their owners' first names: Mike's Cafe, Ed's Superette,
Toby's Feed Barn.

Toby's brother Waldo Giacomini owns a dairy operation — they call them ranches, not farms — at the northwest edge of town. This has been dairy country for half a
century.

A large brick building at the south end of town stands
empty, but the word is that a deposit has been made and
the new owner plans to put shops downstairs and a hotel
upstairs. With 2.5 million visitors coming annually to the
adjacent National Seashore, business could prosper. But the
old building has to be earthquake-proofed first.

David Mitchell, the editor of the *Light*, calls Point Reyes
Station, with a population of 625, "the commercial hub of
west Marin County." The county begins some forty miles to
the south. You are in it once you drive off the Golden Gate
Bridge, heading north out of San Francisco. It is home both
to the prosperous commuters of Mill Valley and to some 250
farms and ranches. Somewhat like the ground beneath, the
human composition of the county rumbles with seismic activity, the underlying social plates meeting and grinding.
Petaluma, in the north-central part of the county, where the

dairying Giacominis first settled, used to be the "Egg Basket of the World." The millions of laying hens have long since played their final roles in soups and stews, but Bio-Bottoms, children's clothes by mail, has arrived. In nearby Nicassio, George Lucas, producer of *E.T.*, has built his studio, dubbed "Lucasland."

This is a county in the which the Peace Commission is boycotting any company affiliated with the nuclear-weapons industry. Because of the boycott, a county supervisor was prevented from renting a Ford to go on county business.

Janet Lipsey came here from Omaha, Nebraska, when her husband got a job as an audio engineer at "Lucasland." A former Montessori teacher, she works part-time at the visitors' center at the National Seashore. She says, matter-of-factly, "I think of West Marin as the state most likely to secede from the nation."

Art Rogers, the town photographer, came to Point Reyes by way of New York City and the Bay Area. He arrived in a Studebaker truck, which doubled as his home until he was able to build a shack, using doors rescued from a dumpster. In a self-portrait from those hippoid days, Rogers and a friend are kneeling in front of Rogers's dwelling, with its six-door facade, proudly displaying the bounty of a mushroom hunt. Rogers is leaner than today, his curly hair untamed. The smile is unchanged, though. The grin still fits the voluble thirty-nine-year-old father, a recent recipient of a Guggenheim Fellowship.

For the last fifteen years, Rogers has been taking photographs of the people of Point Reyes, producing a black-and-white documentary of the town. Despite his unconventional background, Rogers says, "I always worked traditionally." The typical Art Rogers photograph is, he says, "the sharply focused, classical image."

As one looks through Rogers's photographs — the individual portraits, the community groups, the families, the marriages, the ranchers — a general picture of the community emerges. It is roughly made up of equal parts "long-hairs — or former long-hairs — and cowboy hats," to borrow the phrase of Mitchell, at the *Light*. The strong multi-generational Catholic ranching families continue to be viewed as the foundation of the community, but the influx of newcomers is recasting the town.

"In 1971, it was an entirely different town," Rogers says. "Sometimes I think I would like it to be like it was in the early seventies," he adds, "but I know it will never be like that." Then he admits, "If you want to live in a place like this town was in the 1970s, you'd have to move someplace where nobody else wants to be."

Rogers's work provides a record of the town, its mutation. He calls this collected work "The Point Reyes Family Album." Each week, the *Light* publishes an Art Rogers original. "My photography is a way to express positive attitudes," Rogers says. "Maybe it is my way to do things for my community.

"I feel like I grew up here."

David Mitchell came from El Salvador. He originally came here from elsewhere in California, by way of Florida and Iowa, but he went away to cover a war. Then he returned. You might say he came home. His job now as owner, publishers, and editor of the *Point Reyes Light* is, to paraphrase him, to be "an expert on the town." The job pays him about $6,000 a year.

Using the equity from their house after Mitchell was fired from a paper elsewhere in California, Mitchell and his first wife bought the *Light* in 1975 when it was an unprofitable weekly. A few years later, in 1979, the *Light* was awarded a Pulitzer Prize for Meritorious Public Service, the highest award in newspaper journalism. That was only the fourth time in history the Pulitzer judges had so honored a weekly.

The *Light* was cited for a series of investigative reports and editorials about Synanon, the drug-counseling program turned outlaw religious cult. At one point, Synanon had filed suits against the *Light* seeking in excess of $1 billion in damages. Unlike other newspapers in northern California, which had viewed Synanon tolerantly, as another quirk of California culture, or had been scared away from probing Synanon's activities because of the organization's legal attacks, the Mitchells bored in. They were defended in their investigations and outspokenness by more than $1 million worth of pro bono legal counsel provided by the San Francisco law firm of Heller, Ehrman, White and McAuliffe. As the saying goes, "There is no free lunch," and a free press can be costly.

The Mitchells' divorce led to the sale of the *Light,* and David joined the staff of the San Francisco *Examiner.* He had never covered a war — "It was like a hole in my résumé," Mitchell says — and he wanted to. He got his wish; the paper posted him to El Salvador. "It was not what I expected," Mitchell says, which was "excesses by a few — people going to extremes to maintain a semblance of normalcy." Instead, for him, "the revelation about war was the breakdown in normal social controls. People, soldiers, are frightened and angry. What they are capable of under those circumstances is hard to imagine."

But in 1985 the combination of Mitchell's frustration with big-city journalism and the *Light*'s financial difficulties brought Mitchell back to Point Reyes Station, where, as editor of the paper, he believes he has a special responsibility: "If you take a town like this — that is, unincorporated, with no city council — the social agenda, the political agenda are to a large degree directed by this newspaper. It's not that we dream up the ideas. We're listening to all the chatter — to learn the things that public attention needs to be focused on — to focus the community's attention on those things."

Mitchell is a tall, bearded man with a nose that takes a marked left turn. Dressed in blue jeans and a matching jacket, he is sitting with his back to a rolltop desk. "I see myself as a reporter," he continues, "mainly because I think my talent is that I have a good news sense. I recognize when there's something interesting or peculiar going on."

He proceeds to offer an example of an important subject the *Light* brought to west Marin's attention: the boom in the population of Mexicans in the area. According to Mitchell, about three hundred Mexican laborers, mostly men, came into the community in the mid-1970s, the majority to work on ranches in the area. After they had saved some money, they sent for their families. Within a five-year span, the number of Mexicans tripled, and suddenly they made up 10 percent of the local population.

Mitchell says, "The overwhelming issue is: how do you report that? If you report it as hordes of aliens crossing the border into your nice little community, think of the trouble that would have been caused. Well, what we did — this is one of the things I'm as proud of as anything we've done. . .''

Mitchell gets out of his chair in mid-sentence and goes over to a four-drawer file and opens a drawer. He glances up — "Sorry. I thought I could put my finger on it in a second" — and opens other file drawers. Finding what he was looking for, the May 28, 1985, issue of the *Light*, he continues: "I thought this was overwhelming information, and I was afraid if I presented it wrong, I would create tremendous problems for the Mexicans here. So we put together a history of the ethnics immigrating to west Marin."

What the paper showed was that five waves of immigrants have come to settle around Point Reyes: Irish, Swiss-Italians, Portuguese, Yugoslavs, and Mexicans. Further, the articles pointed out that all the Swiss-Italians came from one little valley, all the Portuguese came from the Azores, the Yugoslavs — boatbuilders — were from two islands. And Mitchell concluded: "All the Mexicans are from two tiny villages. We put the newcomers in context."

Proud of not having given in to the facile approach, to attention-grabbing headlines, Mitchell is also determined not to mimic the morbid curiosity of the big-city press. "One of the things I absolutely hated, and it happened all too often, was being sent out to knock on some mother's door and ask, 'What did you think about when the car ran over little Mary Jane's face?' We don't milk the misery of the victims and their families."

Instead, for example, Mitchell says, "We have a seventy-eight-year-old sex therapist who writes a weekly column."

Mitchell explains that he has developed a firm conviction that a source of terrible problems in his parents' generation

was — is — sexual repression. So he asked himself, "If this
is something I feel so strongly about, why don't I do something about it?"

He did. He publishes a column by Dr. Eleanor Hamilton.
"It is the most-criticized thing in the paper. She's also one
of the best things in it. There's a lot of people who say her
column is the first thing they turn to."

As a recent example, Dr. Eleanor Hamilton wrote on sexual communication. She concluded that column: "Anxiety
is communicated through body odor also. Learn to recognize it so that you may dissipate the fear which generates it.
Learn also to know the smell of eager anticipation for love.
Such fragrance says, 'I am waiting for you. Come, let us
share our love.'"

Ernie Spaletta did not come from anywhere else. He has
lived all of his thirty-two years in the same wood-frame
house on the Spaletta Ranch. It is one of eighteen dairy cattle ranches in the 20,000-acre Pastoral Zone that is part of
the Point Reyes National Seashore, located on the peninsula
underlaid by the Pacific Plate. Ernie is a large man, with an
unshaven face that could be described either as covered with
stubble or as distinguished by a close-cropped blond beard.
In a sense, he is a national treasure.

The legislation creating the Seashore was enacted in
1962. With appropriations authorized, the government
bought the ranches on the peninsula and then leased them
back to the ranchers. "The Seashore is not just protecting a
natural system, but a cultural landscape" is how Don Neu-
bacher, chief naturalist (from Sonoma County, California,
by way of Sharon, Connecticut), explains it.

Ranching accounts for 40 percent of Marin County's

economy, and agricultural zoning in Marin calls for sixty-acre-minimum lots. The county government has held firm to its zoning plan, reducing speculative buying and the inflation of land prices. Further working for the survival of the agricultural community is the Marin Agricultural Land Trust, which has acquired easements on 11,500 acres of land, assuring that they will remain in agriculture forever. Other factors have helped keep development at bay: the Seashore and the contiguous Golden Gate National Recreation Area, neighboring state parks, the distance from San Francisco, and the winding roads along the way, the continuing influence of the old-time ranch community, and the strong environmental orientation of the newcomers — this "mosaic of influences," as one person put it.

In the Seashore Pastoral Zone, the land is rolling, with dramatic views of the Pacific Ocean. In the spring, it is green following the winter rains. The climate is described as Mediterranean, and the average temperature difference between winter cold and summer heat is a mere twenty-eight degrees. Although winters are mild, summers on the Seashore are cool and foggy. Wood is dressed in a mossy green overcoat. "People say you get used to the fog, but I'll tell you, you don't," Ernie Spaletta says. "It will be a hundred degrees over in Petaluma, and we'll have the wood stove going."

Also, the salt air is corrosive. Spaletta's neighbor, George Nunes, who has lived all of his fifty-one years on the A Ranch, surrounded on three sides by the Pacific Ocean, says, "If you get eight years out of fence wire, you're lucky."

They milk 320 cows on the Spaletta Ranch, also called the C Ranch because it is the third ranch inland from the ocean-splashed promontory of Point Reyes. Milking, which is largely handled by three Mexicans, starts at 2:30 in the morning and ends at 6:30. The afternoon milking then begins at 1:30.

Typically, farmers in west Marin have bought all their feed, because summers are not warm enough to grow alfalfa or grain. Hay is trucked in from Nevada and California's Central Valley, where they can make six cuttings of alfalfa a season. Nunes does grow 250 acres of oats for silage. "We started with thirty-eight acres in 1974, the wife and I. We were the first ones to do it in this county," he says. Other ranchers have followed suit.

In addition to running the dairy ranch, Spaletta also has a thirty-foot boat, built in 1924, moored at a commercial boat dock in the lee of the point. In season between milkings, he goes fishing for salmon and crabbing for Dungeness crabs. The fishing makes him a few dollars; it is also his recreation. At the suggestion that he give up the dairy business and, to give himself more free time, raise beef, he responds: "No, that's a lazy man's business."

Spaletta's wife, Nichola, immediately remarks: "He works himself to death." Her words and tone, like those of dairy wives around the nation, contain a mixture of admiration and frustration.

The Spaletta Ranch is right on the road to the promontory from which hundreds of thousands of Bay Area daytrippers view the migration of gray whales, north in the early spring from Mexican water, south in the late fall from the Arctic. The ten-thousand-mile migration is the longest of any mammal's. In one two-hour stretch during the height of the migration, 2,900 cars went out to the point. "It's wild here on the weekend," Nichola says. And with three small children to look after, she adds, "I'm a nervous wreck."

Do they have problems ranching on the Seashore?

"No," Nichola responds cheerfully.

"Yes," says Ernie honestly.

Nichola, twenty-seven, a handsome, upbeat woman, is the Spaletta Ranch's head of public relations.

Ernie seems to proceed straight ahead, without guile. He fits the stereotype of the rancher: reserved and hardworking. Independent. Just like George Nunes, who said: "When I was young, I never backed down from anyone or anything."

"The rangers, they bug you," Ernie says.

Later, when Ernie is off keeping an eye on a new hired man who appears an uncertain master of the tractor, Nichola speaks for him. "He's so private. He works so hard, and he feels like they're picking on him. We've never been off the ranch together overnight since the honeymoon [eight years ago], because of his work."

Later Ernie says, "I like it here. I don't mean to say I don't. I've lived here all my life."

Ernie Spaletta: fourth-generation dairyman of Swiss-Italian descent, born and raised on the farm, determined to stay. In 1962 the federal government took him under its wing. That was a mixed blessing.

The Spaletta Ranch is in the public eye — being part of the Seashore, it is owned by the public. As a consequence, Nichola says, "The park rangers make us keep it cleaned up." For example, she says, "If you've got a sick cow, you've got to hide her." Last summer the park management suggested that the Spalettas repaint their house.

Ernie Spaletta, George Nunes, and the other ranchers on the Seashore are subject to a curious combination of protection and interference. They do not have to worry about escalating land prices and taxes, but at the same time, they do have to satisfy their landlord, the Park Service. "They want you to upgrade your place," Nunes says. "They want these places to look nice, but you can't blame them." Nunes is talking about appearances, but he could easily be referring to more than cosmetics.

The Seashore has hired a range manager and is studying whether to restrict grazing in problem areas, where, say, erosion might result. As much as ranching is part of the Seashore's cultural landscape and as much as a pastoral landscape has its own special beauty, public ownership of land and public involvement in agricultural issues have come to mean increased public scrutiny of agricultural practices.

Jules Evens came here from Vermont, where he was raised on a small dairy farm. But he says, "I don't have any romantic attachment to agriculture." Evens is a research associate at the Point Reyes Bird Observatory; some 338 species of birds have been identified in the Seashore. On the screen of his MacIntosh computer is an article he is writing on the decline of black rails. He recently finished writing a book on the natural history of the Seashore. On this afternoon he has been talking about the importance of ranching in the community, but he is concerned about overgrazing, about the damage caused by cows grazing along creekbeds. He is cautious about being critical of ranching; that is a delicate matter in this community. He knows that, but he has one important point to make: "Ranching has to be viable without being subsidized at the expense of the health of the land."

Bob Harris is from Baltimore, by way of graduate school in mycology. "My first month here, I ate twenty-eight species of mushroom. I thought I'd died and gone to heaven," he says. "During mushroom season, the whole town's in the woods."

Harris and his wife, Jennifer Snyder (from Kansas City, Missouri), run Mushroompeople, a business that supplies spawn for shiitake mushrooms to both home gardeners and commercial operators. Shiitake typically are grown on oak logs using plug spawn — wooden dowels, impregnated with shiitake mycelia, inserted into holes drilled in the logs. Mushroompeople also sells sawdust spawn — inoculated sawdust that can be packed into chain-saw cuts in oak logs.

Harris and Snyder, who have spent time in Japan, where shiitake culture is a major industry, grow their own strains of shiitake spawn for sale, but they are not farmers. They are proponents of what Harris calls "laid-back high-tech: we use a computer and burn wood."

In fact, Harris, who attended but did not finish medical school, increasingly is turning his attention to computer projects. He now spends one day a week in San Francisco, where he is helping to develop comprehensive medical software, which will keep track of appointments and billing and help with diagnosis. "We'll drive doctors to the MacIntosh," he boasts. He goes on to note that there are 750 families living around Point Reyes Station and 150 MacIntoshes.

(Bob Volpert, who came from Lake Placid, New York, by

way of a stock-brokerage house, says, "This community has an enclave of Mac users who are cultish in their exuberance." Volpert runs his wilderness-rafting business a few doors away from Harris and Snyder; he relies on IBM clones and confesses — an admission that hints of sacrilege — that he does not care about computers.)

One of the reasons Harris has turned to computer work is that running a small business in a rural community is no easy way to make a living. Besides, Harris says, unhindered by false modesty, "I'm an innovator, a creator."

To his way of thinking, California is the place for someone like him: "It is truly almost a classless society. It doesn't matter how much you had, how much you have, what you own. Back East, they're much more concerned with status — your social background, your economic background. Culturally, California's been a gas. It's the frontier.

"Diversity is its strength."

To hear Harris explain it, Point Reyes is the ideal place to live: "We're not far enough away from San Francisco that we've elected a rural life-style to the exclusion of a cosmopolitan world, but it's not the same as the East Coast — we don't have the traffic, the population density, the congestion. We don't have the drastic winters, so we don't have such a crush at the Seashore in the summer."

"We get four or five months of spring," Snyder adds.

Recognizing that they might be making it all sound too idyllic, Harris throws in a mention of shark attacks at the beach — the last was in the seventies — and poisonous mushrooms growing in the front yard.

Some would also mention the risk of another major earthquake. To those prophets of doom, Harris responds,

"People say, 'How can you live on the Fault?' Let me tell you something: every year all kinds of people back East are killed by lightning.

"We don't have lightning," he says.

"We don't have hurricanes," he adds.

Snyder chimes in, "We just get soft rain."

Pat Healy came from Cleveland, Ohio, by way of Los Angeles, where she left behind a spouse and a career as a jazz singer. She came to Point Reyes Station and took a job as a veterinarian's assistant. Two years later, she got into the restaurant business, because, she says, there was a For Sale sign in the window of the Station House Café. "I thought having a restaurant would be manageable." Now she owns three.

"I've spent a lot of time keeping up with the monster I created. I'm absolutedly amazed that this happened to me. I didn't know I was a business person. I didn't know I could be a leader."

With seventy-five employees working for her, she is one of the biggest employers in the area. A trim woman, she is wearing dark gray sweat pants and a lighter gray sweatshirt. Her eyes are blue — you notice them. Her hair is brown and short, and when she brushes it back, you see the gray underneath.

"I've grown up," she says.

Although her development has been contemporaneous with that of others who arrived here in the seventies, Pat Healy is not their contemporary. She just turned sixty. "One of the things I learn as I grow older is, the most important thing you do is your work. When all is said and done, nothing means as much as the satisfaction of a job well done."

That strikes me a curious — perhaps even retrograde — remark. So many people who chose to resettle in country places chose to do so precisely because they did not want their lives to be weighed by conventional scales, which so frequently means measured by business accomplishments. The urban émigrés wanted fuller lives, spiritual lives, family lives — private lives, or, if you will, internal lives — in addition to public lives, which is to say, business and professional lives. They thought, when they set out from their various narrow and restrictive homes, that they would not be content to sail the narrow channel that had confined their forebears.

And for Pat Healy, business success may indeed be a bold exploration — although it is revealing to see, in her and her Point Reyes colleagues, how the thrill of landfall has given way to the staking of claims.

To be sure, they are not insubstantial claims. Healy has transformed the Station House from a "plain old vanilla burger joint," to cite the reviewer and farmer Orville Schell, into a restaurant celebrated in the culinary press for its local mussels and oysters, its California-grown shiitake mushrooms, and for its organic beef, supplied by the [Orville] Schell-Niman Ranch in nearby Bolinas.

Healy first met Schell, who is justly celebrated for his writings about modern China and, appropriately, the modern meat industry, back when she was working for the veterinarian. Schell brought in his dog Ed, a black Labrador, after the animal had been hit by a car. The vet needed to keep Ed overnight for observation, and Healy remembers that Schell spent the night in the run with his recovering companion. "For years afterward, I confused their names. If I would see Orville on the street, I would say, 'Hi, Ed.'"

She remembers Art Rogers when he was living in his truck. For more than fifteen years, she has watched diners in the restaurant, "watched the evolution of their relationships," as she puts it. "One evening, you see that someone — usually the guy — is having dinner by himself. You'd say, 'What's going on here?'"

Healy calls it "the drama of families."

She has watched as parents have visited their rebellious offspring and brought them to the Station House for dinner. "You would see who they really were, or who they would become," she says, wisely, for who ever completely picks out all the birdshot of childhood influences embedded in us?

"Over time, they have cut their hair, got a job, bought a house. Some of them have become very prosperous," she says. "They've all pretty much settled down and reflect their upbringing."

They seem to have accepted their destiny, Healy suggests. "They are who they were meant to be," she says.

Chapter 13

A VIRGIN NO MORE

PALMER, ALASKA — Ted Pyrah is swearing. His language is not original, but it is vigorous. The man is a master of the percussive Anglo-Saxon monosyllables, giving them a heartfeltness that suggests the expletives are not routine filler, but rather are the meat of the message.

Pyrah, stocky and unshaven, wearing a quilted jacket with insulation spilling from rips, has just dismounted from his three-wheeler in front of a cluttered workshop. The object of his complaint is the Matanuska River, which is now washing across his barley and nugget bluegrass fields and into some of his row crops: potatoes, carrots, broccoli, and cauliflower. The river runs to the east and south of town, through a broad gravel bed edged by willow thickets full of moose and rabbits. Pyrah's farm is across the river from town. About a mile downstream from his place, the Matanuska joins the Knik, which is fed by the Knik Glacier, some twenty miles away. Every year, the Matanuska dumps about three hundred thousand cubic feet of gravel as the river slows and spreads out before its union with the Knik. In July of 1986, the main channel of the Matanuska, filled over time with glacial till, changed course, sluicing eastward through the willows and washing across portions of several farms, Pyrah's among them. In fall, the duck hunting was terrific on the barley field. "It was black with ducks," one hunter remembered. The ducks would fly in and land on the floodwaters, intent on making a meal of the ripe grain. The hunters, using a disk harrow for a blind, made a meal of the ducks. As the water receded, Pyrah scooped salmon fry out of puddles and carried them in buckets to the main channel.

Now Pyrah is swearing because, several years later, the water has risen to its highest levels yet, depositing stumps in the profane farmer's fields.

Pyrah lost his 1986 crop, but the water went down, and he planted the fields in 1987. He lost that crop when the high water came in August. After the water receded, he tried to clean up and cut some ditches to help the drainage. Only his bulldozer got stuck. (Pyrah owns a John Deere 450, which must be the unofficial state pet. There seems to be a bulldozer at the ready in every other backyard in Alaska, which says something about the muscular approach to life up here.) Seeing his $38,000 'dozer with a six-way blade sitting in the mire, Pyrah admitted to being "scared." If the water came up suddenly, the machine could have been entombed in silt.

So Pyrah brought in a logging skidder and had it set up on solid ground. Then the skidder operator hooked the logging cable onto the 'dozer, preparing to haul Pyrah's machine back to safety. Pyrah remembers how the 'dozer would not budge, but the skidder's winch would not quit — as a result, the cable snapped. Pyrah then describes with admiration how, undaunted, the skidder operator walked out into the field, tied a square knot in the one-inch cable (at this point in his tale, Pyrah's thick hands move in pantomime), and tried again. Making a noise like a child inhaling a strand of spaghetti, he cheerily reports the result: "It sucked that 'dozer up like a noodle."

Pyrah figures this latest round of flooding will cost him $25,000. One can hardly resist pointing out the irony that in a year of drought, in Alaska you find a farmer plagued by flood. But then, in Alaska, things are not always the same as they are in the Lower Forty-eight.

"Alaska's raw," Mark Weaver says. It looks as though every car that has ever broken down or crashed in the state is parked in someone's yard. The indigenous architecture is the ramshackle box, the siding of choice, plywood. "The cute gables and cupolas weren't ever built by the first generation," Weaver says.

Lift your eyes above the man-made world, and you see the Chugach Mountains, the Talkeetnas, still snow-peaked in midsummer. Drop your gaze, and the structures of men-in-a-hurry greet you. When the word *surreal*, which means the juxtaposition of incongruous elements, was coined, Alaska was defined.

Weaver and his wife, Beverly Cutler, both in their late thirties and both graduates of Yale Law School, came to Alaska in 1974. She is now a state Superior Court judge, back at work after a maternity leave following the birth of the couple's third child. He is a potato farmer, having been fired as the director the state Division of Agriculture for speaking his mind.

In many respects, Weaver and Cutler appear conventional. Graduates of a prestigious law school, they live in a handsome log house that Weaver built. The judge, trim and attractive, is looking after the children on the weekend. On a cool, rainy day, Weaver is wearing a voguish Patagonia "Synchilla" jacket. They are not typical Alaskan "end of the roaders," people who headed for "The Last Frontier," as the state license plate boasts, because life in the Lower Forty-eight was somehow too confining, because they are misfits or malcontents or terminally shy. They do, however, live where no family has lived before, at the end of one mile of dirt road. "We're five days' drive from anywhere," Weaver says, excluding from his definition of "anywhere" nearby Anchorage, an hour's drive away.

They bought the land from the Matanuska Borough (the county government) in 1977, built their house, and then moved to the farm in 1983. Before coming to the farm, Weaver practiced law in Anchorage, putting all his earnings into clearing the land, which was and always had been for-est. They lived on Cutler's judicial salary. "Farms eat a lot of capital," Weaver says. The land that Weaver planned to farm had never had a single crop grown on it. "Developing these fields was an act of faith. I didn't know what was here. I was clearing the land, looking for a crop, but I didn't know what the crop would be."

With the help of two D-8 Caterpillar bulldozers (and his own John Deere 450), he has so far cleared 60 of the 220 acres he bought. Another 40 acres have had the trees and stumps bulldozed, but they are still a few years away from being ready for planting. For soil, what he found was loess, nutrient-deficient windblown glacial dust. For a crop, he settled on seed potatoes. He rotates fields, planting about 10 acres per year, which gives him a yield of approximately 100 tons of certified (virus-free) seed potatoes. This lawyer, who

never farmed until five years ago and is now farming literally virgin soil, is the largest in-state supplier of certified seed
for one of Alaska's major crops.

"Alaska is one of the last places in the United States that is
a Third World country," Mark Weaver said.
"This is a substantially different state from any other in
the nation," says State Senator Jay Kerttula. "There is no
indigenous economic base, no indigenous equity. We're
more rural and remote than any other state. We have no
surface transportation to speak of."

As he eats a large bowl of oatmeal in a restaurant outside
Palmer, Kerttula is wearing a gray baseball cap from the
University of Michigan, where his daughter earned her doc-
torate. Now in his sixties, Kerttula arrived in Alaska as a
young boy when his parents were shipped up here as part
of the "Matanuska Colony," a farming community established by the Roosevelt administration during the depression. He was a dairy farmer and has been in the state
legislature for more than twenty years.

"Our statehood framers gave us one hundred four million acres of land and their resources, which we cannot
sell," Kerttula says. "The rental of those resources is what
fuels the state's economy. No other state is like that."

Substitute sand for snow, and Alaska becomes an Arab
country. "Oil is king," one businessman says. "Saudi Arabia
is the key to the price of oil — the Saudis control the Alaskan economy." The oil lying under Alaska's surface is extracted   by   foreign — that   is,   Lower   Forty-eight —
companies. "Profits made here go straight out to Houston,
Seattle, New York City," Kerttula says. "The profits aren't
reinvested here."

As Mark Weaver puts it, "We haven't developed a local economy. The interstate commerce clause in the Constitution is the biggest threat to local economy there is. By prohibiting the taxing of imports from other states, it tends to prevent states from protecting their local producers."

The value of oil produced in Alaska in 1986 was $11.3 billion. Fishing was valued at $1.2 billion. The third largest "industry" was, get this, the federal government, which provided $900 million to the state in various ways. Tourism generated $413 million. ("Tourism doesn't create new wealth," Weaver remarks. "It distributes existing wealth.") Forest products were valued at $259 million. Mining, $198 million. Agriculture production is valued at a mere $30 million annually, less than that of a significant county in the heartland. Kerttula comments, "It's a gnat."

Palmer has long been at the center of the state's major agricultural region. A low, spread-out town of several thousand inhabitants, it sits on the west bank of the Matanuska River, some forty miles northeast of Anchorage, the largest city — and hence the largest market — in Alaska. Gravel pits abound, both small Mom-and-Pop excavations and large operations. Every day 160 to 240 train cars, each loaded with 80 tons of gravel (called "Palmer Gold"), go to Anchorage, where most of the available building sites are underlaid with a "miserable deep peat," in the words of one builder. The peat is dug out, the gravel dumped in, and a building can go up.

The Matanuska Valley became the state's agricultural heart as a result of the depression-era program that trans-

planted families like the Kerttulas. The Roosevelt administration's creation of the Matanuska colony was fraught with
failure and idiocy, but with some success as well. Insofar as
agriculture ever took hold in the state, it took hold here,
where summers are mild and winters, if cold, are moderated
somewhat by the proximity to the coast.

With the discovery of vast pools of oil under the North
Slope and the construction of the eight-hundred-mile-long
pipeline (four feet in diameter, with half-inch thick walls)
in the late 1970s, boom times came to Palmer, along with
the rest of the state. It took $8 billion to build the pipeline,
which carries some 84 million gallons a day. With profits
on pipeline oil now on the order of $12 million a day, state
tax revenues went from $333 million in 1975 to $3.26 billion in 1985.

One way the state decided to spend the money was to
expand its agricultural base. So it committed a total of about
$100 million in subsidies and loans; of that, $50 million
went to develop grain production around Delta Junction,
south of Fairbanks in the interior, and $20 million to un-
derwrite a new community of eight dairies on Point Mc-
Kenzie, across the sound from Anchorage. As one observer
commented, the state tried to do overnight what it took generations to accomplish in the Midwest.

The dairies are struggling; several appear doomed. (In
part, Mark Weaver got himself in trouble for saying no extraordinary measures should be taken to rescue the dairies
in peril.) As for the grain-growing region of the delta, the
experience there reveals the kind of foolishness that can result when politicans decide to think big and, to support their
thoughts, spend someone else's money. Some 60,000 acres

of virgin ground were cleared for the growing of oats and, especially, barley. Small grains do reasonably well in Alaska, and the plan was for Alaskan farmers to enter the export market with their crop. But grain prices collapsed, and with them plans for the delta.

Now, less than ten years after the launching of the agricultural-development program, 25,000 acres — almost half of those cleared — have been idled under the U.S. Department of Agriculture Conservation Reserve Program, designed to take highly erodable land out of production. In 1988, with drought in the Lower Forty-eight, Alaska, with ample rainfall, had only 4,000 acres planted to barley in the delta. Despite having spent $100 million to develop agriculture, especially small-grain production, farmers in the state had to import grain.

"The delta didn't have a chance to begin with," Kerttula says, proposing an entirely different solution: "They ought to plant buffalo grass and bring the buffalo back."

With the flaws of their agricultural development plan apparent, the legislature is reluctant to invest more in farming. "By that line of reasoning," comments Frank Mielke, Mark Weaver's successor at the Division of Agriculture, "the Wright brothers would have quit if their first plane had failed. We tried to build a 747 the first time around — a lot of the thinking in Alaska is short-term."

"I think agriculture in Alaska has more potential right now than people give it credit for," Mark Weaver says. "There is nothing in our climate that is a prohibition for agriculture. We have a wonderful climate six months of the year." What grows well are cool-season crops — potatoes, lettuce, cole crops — that like a long photoperiod, which they get during Alaska's almost endless summer days. (June 21, the solstice: a young boy rides his bicycle down the highway at eleven o'clock at night. He is wearing sunglasses.)

Alaska has no Colorado potato beetle, no leaf roller, no late blight. Bill Campbell, who has been developing virus-free seed potatoes for the state, comments "We've got a paradise up here."

"On crops that do well here, we get incredible growth," Weaver says. The seventy-pound cabbages at the state fair in August are legendary — but then, who do you know who wants to put a seventy-pound cabbage in the shopping cart? Carrots do well. (Ted Pyrah sells his culls to the Anchorage Zoo. An elephant eats forty pounds a day, he says; the zoo has two. "Them ol' polar bears eat carrots like popcorn," he adds.) Spinach does not do well; the extended daylight causes it to bolt.

"I look back at our efforts at promoting agriculture," Weaver says, "and most of them have been based on the premise that we could export, but in developing an industry, you have to flow with your market. Our markets are local, Anchorage and Fairbanks. We haven't tapped our markets anything close to what we could."

Although potatoes are a major crop, 50 percent of Alaska's potatoes are brought up from the Lower Forty-eight. "Once we've satisfied our local markets, then we might get that one crop, or two crops, that we can ship." Warming to his subject, he continues: "The history of agriculture up here has been to move Lower Forty-eight methods, Lower Forty-eight crops northward." Alaskan milk produced on the newly developed dairy farms at Point McKenzie is more expensive than milk from California and Washington that has been shipped up. "We haven't worked with things that are naturally adapted."

How about apples? Weaver's wife smiles knowingly. "We grew six apples one year," she reports. "Spring tends to be hard on the trees," he explains.

Seed crops? "Most of the things we can do, Oregon can do better," he says.

"Things that thrive here are different. Cold isn't the critical factor. It's colder in North Dakota. Soil temperature and daylight, those are the things that make the difference. We've got cold dirt. Growth here takes place in the top four inches of the soil. People are always trying to get us to grow alfalfa — it has a fifteen-foot taproot.

"Oil-seed crops grow well — like meadow foam, which yields an extremely high-quality cosmetic oil that replaces whale oil. We may find that there's a cereal crop that does well. We haven't identified all of the possibilities. There's a unique crop somewhere that will be in demand — maybe it's going to be for an industrial application. We need to look to Scandinavia, to China. Why the hell go to Beltsville [the U.S. Department of Agriculture research facility in humid, sweltering Maryland]? You might as well go to Mars."

All the time the oil boom was filling the state's treasury and funding agricultural development, however ill conceived, it was also spurring development in general, which is almost invariably ill conceived. While the delta was being opened up, the Matanuska Valley was being filled up — with local Anchorage commuters and, believe it or not, oil-field workers whose jobs are seven hundred miles away on the North Slope, a two-hour flight from Anchorage.

Typically, those people work for one to three weeks straight and then are off for an equal stretch of time. When they are working, they live in camps built by the oil companies, room and board provided. And when they are off, they definitely do not want to live at the northern reaches of Alaska. Many fly to Anchorage, and then some continue their commute south to the Lower Forty-eight, while others make their homes nearby, which increasingly has meant the Matanuska Valley.

"One of our biggest problems today is the unavailability of good farmland," says the man described as godfather of agriculture in the valley, Paul Huppert, a vegetable grower and the state's largest produce wholesaler.

The inevitable question for anyone from the Lower Forty-eight who has watched development eat up agricultural land is: why didn't the state, which had so much money available, spend some of those ample funds on the preservation of prime farmland in the Matanuska Valley?

The answer to that question explains much about Alaska. "Why should a state that owns a hundred four million acres of land buy development rights?" responds Frank Mielke, sitting in Mark Weaver's former office at the Division of Agriculture. (Pointing to a small bottle of Bufferin left on the desk, he remarks, "Maybe Weaver left those for me.") Those 104 million acres account for the state-owned land only. The federal government owns another 218 million acres; native tribes own 44 million, and individuals have deeds to a pittance, 5 million acres.

In his response, Mielke has offered what was the

conventional wisdom at the time the delta area was being developed. "Buying development rights goes totally against the grain in this state. The prevailing view is that the state ought to be developing this land, putting public land in private hands. "Besides," Mielke adds, touching on a crucial point, "not as many people get rich when the state buys development rights. There is no surveying, land clearing, and so on."

Although Alaskans may pride themselves on their pioneer spirit, there is nothing original about their folly. "Bedroom communities destroy farming. We always put a city on the best farmland," Senator Kerttula says. "We follow the pattern of the Lower Forty-eight. We bring all their mistakes up here and renew them."

"It's like raising a teenager," Huppert says. "You don't learn from others' mistakes."

"The valley's shot," says one observer. "Everybody's greedy."

We know, though, every balloon that rises must come down. These are poor times for the oil industry, irrespective of disastrous spills. From 1986 to 1987, oil revenues going into the state treasury declined by $1.26 billion. As a consequence, these are hard times for Alaska generally, which means that for the present, at least, agriculture in Palmer is stable and the building boom has quieted. Mary Psenak, a realtor in town, says, "In the last year we've sold just one house that wasn't repossessed."

Rex Turner, a developer with a stylish log office building on the highway south of Palmer, is optimistic nonetheless. Several years back, Turner put in Equestrian Acres (or "Snob

Hill," as one woman called it), a subdivision of expensive custom homes on quarter-acre lots outside of town. While new construction of Kentucky Derby Drive, Palomino Lane, and the like has slowed, Turner is planning an even more ambitious project: Pioneer Sky Ranch, fifty-four houses and a paved airstrip on 145 acres of former farmland.

(Turner himself owns two planes, including a Piper Supercub, the Alaska state bird. A trim, erect man, his hands resting on an orderly desk top, he says, "I hunted in Africa in the seventies. Now Alaska is one of the few places left where you can have such adventures. A plane gives you the ability to go places where no white men have ever been.")

Turner believes a combination of elements will fuel Alaska's next expansion: the 1994 Winter Olympics, which he expects to be awarded to Anchorage ("Anchorage is the state's nerve center," he says); the expansion of tourism, possibly including a Japanese-built ski area at Hatcher Pass to the north of town; the rapid growth of fishing, and an increase in oil prices in the early 1990s.

Alaskans live for the booms and ride out the busts. Thirty-five thousand people who came to the state during the good times have left. True Alaskans endure — or most do, although hard times have chased even some of them south. Ted Pyrah is waiting for the river to go down or, better yet, to cut a new channel. His fellow Alaskans are waiting for the next "rush," be it gold, timber, or oil — a spill doesn't count. Alaska has them all, a literal wealth of resources, which makes for the conflict many Alaskans feel: they like the state primitive, but they want to make their financial killing, too. Or, as a banker said: "Alaska's future is ahead of it. It's still virgin. There's money to be made here."

Chapter 14

THE GLORY OF THE KINGDOM

NORTH DANVILLE, VERMONT — Steve Parker's T-shirt is forest green. It says, "High Reach Farm." The color is appropriate, the name suggestive.

High Reach is a tree farm located a few hills north of this small community. Parker grows Christmas trees here and manages several hundred acres of woodland. His aspiration seems modest: to make a living off the land, doing the work himself. What he is striving to do is what those who came before have done, but in northeastern Vermont, even such a humble ambition can be a struggle. To do it by choice — and to stick with it for years — requires determination, a deep reservoir of personal strength. It is one thing to try on a country life in the dressing room of experimentation; it is an altogether different matter to buckle down to such a life day-to-day, to make it a fit.

Parker's old Dodge Power Wagon, its distributor cap tied on with baling twine, has brought us up to a meadow that, until recently, was growing Christmas trees. He shuts off the truck and gets out. In his late thirties, he is unexceptional in appearance, of middling height and build, with light-brown hair. He wears tan canvas pants and metal-frame glasses and has a round, cheerful face. It wears a serious look, though, as Parker explains that he is not sure what to do with this meadow. His uncertainty about a course of action exemplifies to a considerable extent the choices and difficulties Parker faces in coaxing a livelihood from the land. Since cutting off the last of the Christmas trees the previous year, he has been rebuilding the soil, liming it first. On some fields, he spreads manure, for which he barters with a neighboring dairy farmer: firewood and Christmas trees for cow manure. Parker has considered planting this field back to Christmas trees in another two or three years, but he is also thinking about diversifying the operation, putting in several hundred apple trees, about which he admits he has much to learn. Being located in hardiness zone 3, where winters are long and deep, he knows that the climate severely limits his choice of varieties. Red Delicious, Granny Smith, and other popular apples would not prosper this far north. He could grow McIntosh, a North Country favorite. It is susceptible to insects and diseases, however, and its culture typically has included a host of chemicals, leaving Parker with a difficult decision. He points to a handsome hedgerow of sugar maples, which he says he would cut out if he planted apples, thereby improving the air drainage on the site and combating late spring frosts, which can nip the fruit in the blossom. Whatever he decides, he has some time — he can hay the meadow for a couple of years, although he will have to set the mower high so as not to bung up the cutter on the Christmas-tree stumps lurking in the grass.

Neighboring the meadow is a small planting of less than a thousand of the 44,000 Christmas trees Parker has in various stages of growth. These are young trees, several hundred blue-green Fraser fir, a native of the mountains of North Carolina, which Parker says, "makes a gorgeous tree." He also has transplanted wildlings of balsam fir from his woods. "This is balsam country," Parker says. High Reach is on the edge of the Kittridge Hills east of the Green Mountains, at the southern reach of the boreal forest, typically a spruce-fir mix.

Parker remarks that the rows of balsam need to be sprayed with herbicide — simazine. He resisted using herbicides when he started growing Christmas trees, but he finally concluded he had no choice if he was going to make a living at it. The trees are in the ground for seven to ten years, competing with sod the whole time. Although Parker has experimented with mulches to suppress weedy competition, he has concluded, "I can't imagine using mulch on a field basis in a large planting." Too time-consuming. Although Parker believes he does more mechanical brush and weed control than many Christmas-tree growers, the extra labor driving up his costs, he still sprays herbicide under the trees.

Parker's cohort in the country is largely of the "organic" persuasion, and he describes the decision to apply poisons as "traumatic." He says: "The family did not want herbicides used on the land. As ambivalent as I feel about them, there's no question that they are necessary." He speaks in an even voice with a steady note of self-possession.

Besides, there is no special market for organic trees. "No one gives a hoot about that," Parker says. He adds that growing trees organically would double the time it takes for them to reach market size. By inference, their price would have to double. And if, unlike the growing interest in organic produce, there is no swelling demand for organic trees, Parker would simply bring an overpriced commodity to the market.

He gets from $12 for fast-growing Scotch pine to $16 for Fraser fir. He has been selling 2,500 to 3,000 trees a year, but is planning to increase that number to 4,000 annually within two or three years. Consequently, he has ambitious plans to get new trees into the ground: 2,000 in the fall and three or four times that many the following spring.

Harvest takes place, according to Parker, "early enough to beat the snow and late enough to mean fresh trees," typically from early November to Thanksgiving. He sells only wholesale. "I've decided I'm a farmer. I'm not in the marketing business," he says. "I know saying that will raise hackles. People say farmers have to become better marketers, but to add marketing and still do justice to your farm, that's a real challenge."

The field in which we have been standing is bordered on one side by a plantation of white pine put in by Parker's father. The Parkers bought the farm in 1953, when Steve was three years old. They were back-to-the-landers twenty years before homesteading was fashionable. Before moving to this part of the world, Parker's father was an editor of a small newspaper in Westchester County, New York, today an executives' ghetto. The cost of a dairy farm in northern Vermont won't put a roof over your head in Westchester.

"They didn't know a thing about what they were doing when they came up," Parker says, "but they worked awfully hard. My dad planted a lot of trees" — more than two hundred thousand, by Parker's estimate. He became a dairy farmer, and, like his father before him, a minister. He died when Parker was sixteen.

Parker did not decide to husband the family land until

he was in his late twenties. After college in the early seventies, he worked in Philadelphia at a center for conflict resolution and principled nonviolence. While there, he met Susan Terry, a woman thirteen years his senior, whom he would marry. She continues to teach and maintain a private practice in conflict resolution and mediation. A native of Louisiana, she has been, in Parker's words, "a really good sport" about adjusting to the farm, the house (still unfinished after ten years), and the deep-wintered North. One brisk morning after Parker and Terry first moved up to the farm, a voice on the television greeted the nation with the announcement, "Good morning, America. It's thirty-five below zero in Saint Johnsbury, Vermont" — a small city less than ten miles away from North Danville. Within moments, the phone rang. It was Susan Terry's mother, asking in plaintive southern tones, "Honey, what are you doin' up there?"

When they came to Vermont in 1976, Parker, perhaps not unlike his father almost twenty-five years before him, was a man in transition. Although he admits he was "fuzzy" about precisely what he would do, he says, "I was determined to keep at it and succeed." In 1986, he was named the Conservation Farmer of the Year in his district, the first time someone other than a dairy farmer had been awarded the honor.

Parker comments: "Sometimes I feel guilty when I think of the condition the world is in, and I realize I walked away from that. But I have an enterprise here that I've taken responsibility for, and I'm going to do the best job that it's in my ability to do. And I've done that.

"Everybody's choice is different, but I feel good about the one I've made. I've gotten a stronger appreciation for how important agriculture is, and there's no need to be apologetic for choosing it."

The Power Wagon bumps through an opening in the pines, and Parker stops at the edge of a field that his father had planted in red pine. The trees were logged in 1982, and the field was left rough. After five years, Parker decided to spend $1,600 to have a bulldozer remove and bury the stumps and level the field. Then he sowed a timothy and clover mix to rebuild the soil. "You can always plant trees on poorer soil, but I hate to see the land on a downhill slide," he says.

Initially, one's instincts suggest that an advantage of tree farming over, say, dairy farming is that trees require less attention than cows. There is truth to that notion. Healthy trees do grow without a lot of help from man and without the attentions of a veterinarian, and they do not have teats that require tugging twice a day. Nonetheless, Parker, like all good farmers, is manipulating the growing environment. Agriculture is not a natural state, and Parker is domesticating a feral landscape. As we round a bend, the reasons for that become evident.

Wildlings — or volunteers that reseeded from an earlier planting of Christmas trees — randomly dot the hillside. "They're ungodly to maintain," Parker says. When shearing trees to shape them or when mowing weeds, "you have to go here and there, and up and down." Not the ergonometric ideal. In addition, trees that are shaded grow unevenly; those in wet pockets do poorly. Although the seedlings obviously come at no cost to the grower, maintenance is an uncommon chore.

When the last of these trees is harvested in the next

couple of years, Parker is thinking about letting this area
return to forest. He would like to replant it with a good
timber species, but he is not sure what would do well. Cedar
would, but the financial return might not justify the investment. There are pockets that are too wet for white pine to
thrive in. He has considered tamarack, or larch; it has little
commercial value today, but Parker has spoken with old-
timers who admire it, especially its rot resistance. Who can
guess what its value would be at harvest-time, generations
and another century away?

No decision has to be made today. That is often true
when farming with trees, especially those grown for sawlogs. The crop takes a long time developing, and if the right
thing to do is not immediately evident, the farmer/forester
can ponder the situation a bit longer. More damage is likely
to be caused by rushing into action than by holding off for
a while — which in a woodlot can be years.

About sixty acres of High Reach Farm are in the Christmas-tree rotation. Hundreds of its acres, which we are now
bumping through, are forest — woodlot, that is. The road
we are on bisects Parker's father's plantings of white pine
and white spruce, both of which Parker thinned last winter.
The snow closed the road, so he snowshoed in with his saw
to do the cutting in the dense, twenty-year-old stands. Poles
lie every which way on the ground, but soon they will rot
down. In the spruce stand, Parker has piled some of the
thinnings; ruffed grouse, known locally as "partridges," and
hares will take cover in the brush heaps.

"I love working in the woods in the winter," Parker says.
I share his sentiment. It is quiet and still under the snow-
weighted canopy of evergreens, the hush broken by the
saw — cutting quickly through a five-inch pine stem. There

is satisfaction in dropping a tree to give its neighbor room to grow. Yet in the dark of the forest, there is the numbing cold and the difficulty of moving through the deep snow. And always in the woods, especially in dense evergreen stands, there is the frustration that comes when trees you are felling get hung up in those that are left standing. Working in the woods combines the purity and peace of being alone outdoors with the trials that go with hard, physical work, and if you succeed at all, the pleasure is all the greater for the setting in which your accomplishment takes place.

Sometimes the government will pay Parker a small per-acre subsidy, an inducement, to do so-called timber-stand improvement, but the activity's virtue, like that of any weeding, is its benefit to the crop that follows.

Parker's tactics for weeding his hardwoods, primarily sugar maple, along with some yellow birch, have been different. Reliable neighbors have culled poor trees for firewood. They buy the standing timber, paying approximately $30 a cord, and cut and remove the wood themselves. "The firewood market is just a great tool for improving a woodlot," Parker says, and he has used much of the revenue from it to build roads through the woods. The one we are walking on has recently been put in at a cost of more than $2,000, with the Soil Conservation Service contributing about half of that cost. The road includes a large culvert, so that skidders no longer have to churn through a stream. To combat erosion of the roadbed, it has been seeded with winter rye, which comes up quickly until a conservation mix of grasses and clover takes hold permanently.

Under Parker's eye, "thousands of thousands" of board feet of sawlogs have been taken out of the woods. Parker checks logging jobs daily and, as a rule, has been happy with the work loggers have done. When work has gone badly, Parker says, "I would be more critical of myself than I would be of the loggers."

Loggers are, of course, usually portrayed as the villains in forestry tales, and logging has been the chosen occupation of more rough characters than of college graduates. Woods work is hard and dangerous — most country occupations are. The pay is based on production, the number of board feet cut and skidded and trucked. Ineffable qualities do not earn bonuses. Parker thinks that one common problem on logging sites is that a forester and logger's standards of acceptable work are usually different from a landowner's: "One sees it every day of his life, the other only once." Those who make their living in the woods know that trees along the skid trails will get barked, that slash — tops and limbs — will be spread around the forest floor, that some ruts and muddy spots will be left behind unless the work is done in deepest winter. All logging cannot be done then, though, not if we want wood for our floors and furniture and so forth, not if we expect men to earn a living in the woods.

Not long ago, Parker decided to clear-cut a ten-acre stand of spruce in which all of the trees were the same age and size. The decision to clear-cut did not come easily to him. After a so-called selective cut in a mature stand, in which only some of the trees are harvested, there is a danger of blowdown among the trees left standing. With some of their protection gone, the stems of the remaining older spruce might snap in a strong wind; their bunched root systems might give way. Thinning is best done while trees are young.

Parker admits, "I've wrestled with this, but I think it was a good decision to clear-cut. We've got a fresh start."

He has replanted white pine and white spruce on eight-foot centers, after going through with a brush cutter and mowing narrow rows. The brushy growth on the site will shade the seedlings, deterring the pine weevil, a problem in young stands of white pine. The insect bores into the tree's leader, killing it, causing a side branch to turn skyward and take over as leader. The following year, or two or three later, this replacement leader can also be weeviled, causing another side branch to take the lead, in a sort of shifting formation like geese on the wing. The result is a bushy tree, with no straight stem from which boards can be milled. "Cabbage pine" is the disparaging term for such billowing specimens.

For Parker, the woodland is not a park. It is land to be worked. He makes decisions that alter and — from a commercial standpoint — improve the forest. He also knows those decisions affect wildlife, and he can — and may — make choices that improve their habitat as well. But he has no misgivings about exerting control over the forest.

"Before I got involved full-time in farming, I was an environmentalist," Parker says. "Environmentalism has been an urban view of the world. It has been a reaction to seeing a lot of the abuse that has occurred. It says the ideal view of nature includes no human presence at all. But there is an extensive human presence."

Certainly man will make his mark if we intend to have people continue working in our fields and forests. That mark need not, however, be a scar. "There is an explosion of information about what's good forestry," Parker says. "It's regionally adapted. There are all the data necessary for a landowner to determine, for example, how much of the canopy to open up to get yellow-birch germination or sun-loving varieties. You can determine what kind of stand you'll have in twenty-five years based on what kinds of practices you use now.

"I see what I think is a real degradation of timber stands around here because of cutting practices. I think if people knew about the information that's available, you'd get a lot more good stewardship of the land."

The forest of the Northeast is an important one. The mix of hardwoods is spectacular — sugar maple, red maple, white birch, yellow birch, black birch, white ash, white oak, red oak, shagbark hickory, pignut hickory, cherry, butternut, basswood. That does not include the elms, both red and white (or slippery and American), which are dying out, or hop hornbeam, which is of no commercial value but which grouse and turkeys feed on and which makes terrific firewood. Not only are these woods of great economic importance, so too are the small private woodlots on which they grow. Of 483 million acres of timberland in this country, only 136 million are public land, much of it federal and most of that in the West. Private industrial timberland — owned by Boise Cascade, Georgia Pacific, Weyerhaeuser, and such — accounts for 71 million acres. That leaves 277 million acres, more than half of the forest land in the country, held by individuals. Many of them are absentee owners, often people who see their woodlands not as timber stands but as some kind of haven. Steve Parker, his muddy boots tramping his own ground, is showing the way to the sensitive and prudent management of these important forest lands.

Parker pulls the Power Wagon in next to the barn and parks beside the new logging winch that he will be using in future timber harvests. He will hook it up to a recently acquired 57-horsepower, four-wheel-drive Belarus tractor. New, the Soviet workhorse cost him less than $7,000, probably a third of what it would have cost him to buy green or blue or red — John Deere, Ford, Case/International. Parker admits to having a conservative nature; he dislikes debt. His wife says, "I'm frequently the risk taker. He is so practical, so down to earth. I jostle his steadiness." She urged him to get the tractor.

Having two incomes helps. Since Terry has built up her list of clients, they live on her earnings and plow Parker's revenues back into the farm. "Having her income has enabled me to go the extra mile," he says. "I'm getting to the point where I'm confident about some things. To me, this is a really exciting time to be doing what I'm doing, and I want to be doing the same thing thirty years from now." As his wife notes: "He is a completely happy man."

Happiness is — or has been — a curious notion for this part of the world. North Danville is in Caledonia County, one of the three counties in Vermont's Northeast Kingdom, a scenic outback better known for economic deprivation, sheer hard-bitten poverty, than pastoral joy. It can be a constricted and sometimes twisted world: Orleans County to the north has the highest rate of child abuse in the state.

It is an elemental world, where the roofs are of unpainted metal and steep, designed to shed snow. Even though galvanized, more than a few are rusting. The architecture is spare, yet handsome, the paint white. Along dirt roads, the lattice under the porches is often disintegrating, the trim boards losing the fight to rot.

Wallace Stegner, an elder statesman of American letters, has vacationed in the Kingdom for years, and back about the time Steve Parker was returning home, Stegner wrote of his summering ground: "Vermont is a great character mill, and it grinds exceeding fine. It is too rough a country for pretenders, but it will make room for anyone, however odd, if he doesn't put on airs or show himself incompetent or think himself above the homespun and the calluses and the hard-mouthed virtues that Vermonters have come to the hard way, and don't intend to lose."

As Steve Parker says: "There's a stigma against wealth — the attitudes that go with it. People respect those who work hard."

Merle Gadapee is pushing eighty. A short, trim man, he was a dairy farmer from 1929 to 1973. He started with six cows and was milking forty when he quit and his son, Bruce, took over. He lives alone, now, in the oldest house in town.

These days he sometimes helps Bruce at Bruce's small mill. Bruce sold his cows in the government's whole-herd buyout a few year's back; now he hopes to make a living doing custom sawing. As he eases a hemlock log through the hundred-year-old-mill, his father and a hired man tail the saw — lift off the rough-sawn lumber and stack it on a trailer.

Briefly, Merle plays the comic, reciting a lengthy verse about an old man losing his memory. He says tailing a saw was one of the first jobs he had as a boy. I ask about his days farming. Merle replies: "Ignorant farmers, I'm telling you. Work all day, seven days a week, and wouldn't get so much as a fellow working in a shop." He takes one end of a hemlock slab and dumps it in a trailer.

"But you enjoyed it, though, didn't you?" I ask. (This is what we are supposed to believe, isn't it?)

"Can't say as I did. Four o'clock in the morning to seven o'clock at night, that isn't very common sense, is it?" He grabs a one-inch board and stacks it.

"Why'd you do it?"

"Had to eat," Merle says without a hint of a smile. He hefts his end of a three-inch-thick bridge plank.

After Merle is done with his work, I stop by his house, where he explains that in addition to farming, he always held a second job. He trucked milk for twenty years, lumber after that. "As I say," Merle repeats without a trace of humor, "a fellow can't be too bright to do things like that."

"Were you proud of your work?

"Just showed I wasn't settin' around — and showed I didn't have too many brains."

The following morning at the mill, Merle, the little fingers on both hands misshapen by arthritis, is back at work tailing the saw.

"How are you this morning?" I ask.

"Same old rut, just gettin' deeper," he replies — but with a grin this time. Then, between dumping slabs and stacking planks, he recounts the story of an old farmer who is dying. The farmer tells the doctor that when he goes, he wants to be buried with his Ford tractor, with its chains on. "Why's that?" the doctor asks. Dying farmer: "Cause I ain't never been in a hole it couldn't get me out of."

Merle is the kind of elfin old-timer that the summer people or newcomers tend to coo over, make into a "pet native," to borrow a term from Mary Prior, who grew up in North Danville proper, which is not a town, actually. It is a bend in the road, a dozen white frame houses, one farm in the middle, and a school. The school used to go through the eighth grade; today it is K-2. Tomorrow? Necessary work on the building, especially to meet state codes, will be expensive. As a member of the building committee said, "We can't let sentiment overrule economics." So the young children may soon go to school in Danville, eight miles south. Mary Prior is chair of the Danville School Board. She is known to speak her mind. Her heart too.

Coming to North Danville, I had wanted some place to be spared the onslaught from the outside, wishing that some part of Vermont might still be the state Wallace Stegner described a decade ago. It is, however, becoming this warped hybrid, part suburb, part playground for the cities of the Northeast, the Parkers and Gadapees notwithstanding. Its citizenry seems destined to be composed of the outwash of New York City, where the average lifespan of a tree is seven years. It will fill up with "life-stylers," seeking something more than is offered by the suburbs of New Jersey and Connecticut and making bedroom towns here when they decamp. Its leading citizens will be the resort developers, who are turning the Green Mountains into an amusement park, and their camp followers. There will be just enough young chambermaids to scrub the toilets at the inn — and a few pedigreed old Yankees, lean and taciturn, to plow the driveways in their rusting pickup trucks.

Mary Prior, in her early forties, is a Proud Native, and she starts calmly enough: "My age group that moved here from urban areas did not support the concept of community that I had always known. Many are professional people, people we needed to support the community." She says that the newly arrived parents seemed worried their children would fall behind "their urban cousins who are studying third-year violin in second grade, and French." She is bothered, moreover, by the number of students who were pulled out of the public high school and enrolled in private schools, "because what we had was not good enough. We felt threatened.

"My friends' parents cared as much about me as they did for their own children," she continues. "And that's what we can't understand — how someone could care more about their own children than the community of children. When I was a child, there was none of this putting someone above someone else. I want the best for my kids, but never at the expense of any other child."

The dispute is familiar in rural towns. In some respects it is more about the purpose of education than the importance one attaches to it. That is, is education mastery of an academic discipline, or does it have more to do with understanding people? Is individual achievement more important than community cohesion? Is it better for a high school to offer advanced physics or an unpasteurized mix of contemporaries?

A tremor in Mary Prior's voice: "They can't understand us — I hate that *they/us* — and we can't understand them."

It is the familiar, perhaps inevitable, paradox of the newcomers: how they tend to destroy — damage, at least — the qualities that attracted them somewhere in the first place: the environment, the closeness of the community, the culture. One must be careful not to romanticize poverty and isolation, but one should be equally careful about committing cultural imperialism. It can be accomplished without helicopter gunships and marines.

"Anger, yeah, anger," Mary Prior admits. "I feel I tried to understand, but they don't. They act like we're very ignorant. I get resentful."

Outside of town, a young dairy farmer tells me, "Too many people are moving in." He says the "flatlanders" — nonnatives — used to speed down the road his farm is on. So he put stones in their path. Not boulders, but stones big enough to jar the front end of a stylish import — a Saab, say, or a Volvo — hustling to the office.

The glaciers have blessed Vermont with an infinity of stones. Many of them are the right size for road duty. That would be a good use of an abundant natural resource. Ethan Allen, perhaps the most famous Vermonter of all, came from somewhere else, so perhaps history teaches us that we should stop short of erecting roadblocks. But if one's passage through this rocky, cold, spare state is like running an obstacle course, that's fine. That's the way it has always been.

Chapter 15

SUBURBAN FEVER

STILLWATER TOWNSHIP, NEW JERSEY — Interstate 80 heads west from the Hudson River. You just put the dove-colored smog at your back, traverse eleven states and 3,054 miles, and you're in San Francisco. I'm not headed that far. I've left the interstate at County Road 517 in Allamuchy.

For most of us, our image of New Jersey derives from the acrid corridor in the northeastern part of the state, over which New York City casts its dark, mean shadow. The New Jersey we love to hate is a stifling concrete and asphalt heat sink, with air that can melt your nose hairs. The water is often a carcinogenic brew simmering just beneath the surface, but it was once purified by vast and teeming wetlands. They have since been filled with the metropolitan area's literal trash and sundry figurative refuse, including, according to some reports, the body of Jimmy Hoffa. One can't help feeling that if the rumors are true, the disappeared union boss has been brought to a suitable resting place, embalmed in the septage of subterranean northern New Jersey.

Others have also found Tranquility in New Jersey. Simply follow route 517, and it is the first town you come to in Sussex County, in the northwestern corner of the state. Here the land, like most rural land in the Northeast, is hilly and wooded; the active cropland is planted to hay and corn, with Holsteins out to pasture. The unworked land gives way to weed trees like cedar. Possum lie flattened by the roadside.

Beyond Tranquility lies Stillwater. Stillwater Township is in the "lake country of New Jersey." (That's a bit like describing parts of Iowa as "Little Switzerland," but everyone is looking for the thing that sets him apart from the crowd.) Swartswood Lake, at a respectable 535 acres, is the largest; also in the township are Fairview Lake, Lake Kathryn, Lake Plymouth, Catfish Pond, a couple of others too small to be named on the county map, and part of Paulinskill Lake. The glaciers are responsible for the rocky uplands in Stillwater, where stone walls run back to nowhere in the woods. The farmers who laid the walls are gone. So, too, are their farms.

The township has no town center, no place to shop. It has three small post offices and two volunteer fire departments. Is Stillwater its own place, or is it notable for what it is not?

Joe Connor and his wife and two sons moved to the area in 1980, several years after he bought a condemned 1780s farmhouse set just off the road up a short gravel drive. He is eager to show visitors around the place. In fact, Connor is never so animated as when he is discussing his house. He sets his eye up against a door to show me how to see the marks of the original hand planing. He proudly points to his wife's stenciling, which runs around the top of the wall in most rooms. Connor did all the wrought-iron work for hinges, and on the anvil that now sits on the floor in a corner of the kitchen, he, like the tradesmen who built this house some two hundred years ago, pounded small blocks of iron into nails. Downstairs, Connor has left a small rectangular opening in the plaster, revealing the original split-oak lath beneath. And upstairs in son Devon's room, he has installed a window looking in on the attic, allowing a viewer to see the original workmanship of the pegged roof rafters.

Connor, who once taught sculpture in Hartford, Connecticut, has not sculpted for a number of years. Mastering the craftsmanship required to remake the house fulfilled his sculptural needs, he says: "When I started working on this house, it was so three-dimensional."

Outside on the lawn beside the house are four white gravestones. At first glance, it looks as though the $24,000 purchase price for the house and 7-plus acres included the remains of earlier occupants. Closer inspection reveals the date on each gravestone to be May 4, 1970. Something odd here. Odder still is the cause of death carved on one stone: "A breakdown in communications." The place of death reveals all: Kent State. Connor, a Vietnam veteran, a noncombatant, has moved some of his sculpture to Stillwater with him.

All around the outside of the house are other "found objects," nothing artistic here, but more the sort of scattering that has long been the hallmark of ordinary — that is to say, untidy — country places. Three cowboys boots lie in the driveway. Three empty beer kegs sit next to five worn tires. There's an old bicycle missing a front wheel, a Brownie camera, some rusted fifty-five gallon drums, two rotary mowers that are unlikely to start on the first pull — or any subsequent pull, for that matter — a metal sink, a porcelain mate, rusted bed-springs, flue tiles, and a down-on-its-luck, brown-fading-to-orange Luv pickup. Where chrome letters once spelled "Chevrolet," they now read "MIKADO."

In his junk, as in his work, Connor is an entertainer. He produces concerts and festivals, and a year ago, he wrote arranged, produced, and directed a rock video in which he appears as the lead singer. It opens in black and white; a grandmotherly sort is saying good-bye to relatives, who head off in a 1957 Pontiac. They drive away, and suddenly it's full color, with Grandma in leathers leaping onto a Harley Davidson.

Connor, in shades, wearing a sleeveless blue-jean jacket and a black Harley headband, is singing about the "children of the road." The video has six hundred motorcycles in it: "Speed is our word." In his early forties, Connor is hoping *Rumblin' Thunder* might help to launch him. Even though the extras in the video are almost clean cut, with no tattoos and mouths full of white teeth, Connor's is hardly the sort of tune you would expect from a Republican mayor in a small town.

Then, of course, many small towns today are hardly what you would expect from a small town.

"I know I make a difference," Connor says, explaining why he is active in Stillwater politics. Environmental issues — local ones like that across the street — are what prompted him to seek office. On the other side of Owassa Road is Mountain Shadows Lake, a "condominium campground," or, in the everyday American tongue, a trailer park. A couple of years ago, 250 thirty-feet-by-sixty-feet lots were leased for ninety years for $15,000 apiece. As is so often the case, the owners of the place live out-of-state, happy to foul someone else's nest, and they are talking about expanding the campground. Connor explains that the trailer park sits on what formerly was, according to the definition of the federal government, a "critical wetland." He has doubts that expansion of the trailer park is a good idea.

"For Stillwater to remain the picture I had in my mind, I had to take responsibility to get involved," the mayor explains. His words could comfortably fit in the mouths of small-town residents all over the country. In resort towns, quiet summer places, and once-remote locales just beyond the urban fringe all over the Northeast, the upper Midwest, the Rocky Mountains, and the Pacific Coast, the migrants have arrived. The best of them have valued the special qualities of the "unspoiled" locale — but, in arriving, they have undermined the specialness. Some of them have fought to hold onto the indigenous qualities, sometimes out of goodness, a genuine new-found affection for their communities and for the character of their spot. Sometimes, though, they have fought out of a mean-spirited compulsion to reserve the place to themselves, as though, following their arrival, they had an exclusive claim on it, a right to lock the gate now that they were inside the refuge.

All Joe Connor knows is that the view from the front door isn't what he envisioned when he put aside his art and painstakingly restored the old farmhouse.

Westward out the back door, however, the press of incivility seems remote. The vertical rock outcropping of the Kittatinny Ridge looms at the edge of Connor's property a thousand feet away. It is home to at least one black bear, which got into Connor's beehives and deposited its spoor on the lawn. The top of the ridge, several hundred feet up, is federal land now, protected. Beyond Connor's orchard, which, to be honest, is in about the same shape as the MIKADO pickup truck, saplings reclaim the land. Looking to the west, from the vantage point of his hand-hewn house, Connor can see time reversing itself, an absence of man and the woods growing up. The bear thrives.

But when he looks to the east, Connor sees that he is, literally, up against the wall. Interstate 80 has opened up Sussex County to the commuters. An hour's drive or less gains you the commercial and industrial establishments on the eastern side of New Jersey or puts you on the George Washington Bridge, spanning the Hudson River, to New York City.

Connor has nowhere to retreat as the city — all the inseparable cities strung along the Hudson — advances toward his front door. Or perhaps I would be more accurate in saying this movement toward Stillwater, this "advance," is in truth a retreat. As I listen to some newcomers, I hear an escalating round of urban horror stories explaining why people moved west. The tales begin with personal accounts of rudeness, followed by secondhand stories of theft, mugging, assault, rape, murder — and declining property values. People explain their migration to Stillwater in a transparent code, referring with false disappointment to "urban blight" or speaking with feigned anguish about "a bad experience." One woman, unschooled in euphemism, is straightforward about why she left the city: "Because I got surrounded by niggers."

According to the new town master plan, "rapid conversion of seasonal dwellings to year-round residences" accounts for much of the growth during the past decade. Almost 90 percent of the population growth in the last decade has come from migrants, and the gentrification of Stillwater is progressing nicely. Take driveways, not your standard measure of status, but a revealing one in small places in transition. There are no official statistics under this heading, but my own informal survey of Sussex County residents reveals that newcomers are four times more likely to pave than long-time residents, who are content with natural, utilitarian gravel.

Stillwater has twenty-one miles of county roads; fifty-five of township roads; some of those, like Possum Hill, are, like some driveways, still gravel. For the time being, these provide the kind of rough passage just shy of hardship that the country has been known for. They slow a driver's life appropriately. On gravel roads, errant stones may crack windshields, so the wise proceed at a sensible pace. Gravel roads provide a reminder of what a sensible pace is.

Because Stillwater has no state highways running though it, it is not as convenient a launching pad for commuters as neighboring townships served by Routes 94 and 206. As a result, the population boom may not blow the lid off the township; it is more likely that the lid will simply be lifted gradually, as if by a soufflé rising, the excess ingredients spilling messily. To a modest degree, the new master plan tries to control the heat and the mess by dictating 3-acre-minimum building lots, up from 1½ acres — see if you can get a real-estate salesman to smile as he explains this to you.

Not surprisingly, waste is a problem. Sewage from individual houses doesn't percolate in the ledgy ground; it descends to bedrock, then runs downhill. Polluted wells have been reported, and the master plan notes: "The Paulinskill has little or no capacity to accept additional waste materials without adversely affecting the water quality in the stream."

It is an extraordinary phenomenon, this fouling of the

nest. "We had the cleanest water in New Jersey," Joe Connor says.

As you look around Sussex County, the dramatic, dispiriting evidence of some uncontrollable drive — is it for mere self-gratification? — presents itself immediately in the architectural anarchy of developments. Here, a ranch on a slab, there a Greek Revival–ish thing. The landscape, in response to the developer's cutting, sends up a bloom of residential pustules. Presumably that gambrel-roofed creation derives from barn design, but what possibly can explain a red-tile-roofed Spanish Mission simulation nearby? Was it concocted in a fit of night sweats by a feverish architect? Or could it be the work of some homesick builder longing for the sunshine of San Somewhere in southern California? What explains these irruptions? These "custom" homes have no link to local custom, to indigenous traditions of design or materials or use. In erecting these misconceived structures, we ignore our heritage. We disfigure the land, disrupt society, and wound nature.

At the southern edge of the township, on County Road 521, Don Sharp works the township's last dairy farm, which, like most farms in the county, looks hard used. Don, a self-described "gimp" with a sorry left knee, is assisted by his cousin Tim Gibbs, a handsome man in his twenties.

Don is not a big man. He has still got black hair, but the sideburns are gray now. He is wearing rubber boots and a faded green shirt, snapped at the neck. His blue bill cap reads "Stillwater Supply," but Don goes out of the county for feed and such. The prices have risen near home, which is what happens when working cows give way to recreational horses.

Don never married. "Too busy, I guess," he says. His knee forced him to quit farming in 1981. He sold off the herd, except for one cow, now fourteen, that he still milks. Her horns swirl down like curls above her eyes. "I couldn't let her go," he says. Then a couple of years ago, he started back into dairying — with four cows.

Today, Tim hooks thirty cows — a small dairy herd — to the milking machine. After the machine's cups are removed from a cow's teats, Don strips out the last of the milk by hand. He sits on a three-legged brown metal stool, his head resting in the flank of the cow. A tail swishes his hat askew, but still his hands expertly manipulate the teats, and fine streams of milk shoot into the stainless-steel bucket.

The image presents a small, poignant piece of agricultural history, almost like a black-and-white photograph suddenly come to life, the farmer genuflecting before his animal, the forces of change not merely arrested but reversed. For a moment, the world feels like a better place, almost a good place.

Don finishes the cow he is milking, and, to compensate for the weakness of his game knee, he grabs her tail and a neighbor's, and he hoists himself up. He comes to Buffy, whose horns were the envy of a New Yorker who happened to stop by one day. The guy wanted to buy the horns and mount them on the mantel. "She's got a perfect set of horns," Don says, nodding his head enthusiastically. "Ain't they something?" he adds, appreciatively. Unlike his city visitor, Don thinks horns look best on cows.

"He loves his cows," Tim says, smiling, "loves farmin'." Tim has strong features, a solid build, sandy hair, and a light mustache. He wears a green cap, unadorned by any logos — when was the last time you saw a farmer wearing a hat that didn't double as an advertisement for feed or seed or machinery or chemicals? The short sleeves of his denim shirt are rolled up two turns.

Tim only recently signed on with Don. He gave up a job as a maintenance man at an apartment complex to join his older cousin, a decision that does not altogether please his wife. "She don't like the smell of farming," he remarks, with a cock of the head and slight grin.

After milking, the men go inside for a breakfast of eggs, boiled potatoes, ham, toast, blueberry muffins, and hot chocolate. "Mom," Don's eighty-five-year-old mother, is in charge. She is in stocking feet, with gray woolen leg warmers. Her silver-rimmed glasses tilt slightly upward to the left, giving her a perpetually cocked expression. It suits her. "Do you want cream and sugar," she asks, "or will you drink your coffee barefoot?"

She tells jokes, but the biggest laughs are reserved for the tale of the farmer — with forearms the size of hams, judging by Don's gestures — who was pulled over by a state trooper and told to clean up the manure that had spilled onto the road from the spreader hitched behind his tractor. The farmer agreed he would, but first, he said, he was going to spread his load of manure. No, the trooper said, first clean up your mess. Well, they went back and forth, trooper and farmer, authority versus independence, and then the farmer, still in his tractor seat during the whole exchange, simply hit the hydraulic lever and dropped the bucket loader — bam! — right down on the driver's side of the cruiser.

The trooper couldn't get out his side of the car, but he could radio for help. Turns out the farmer spent a few hours behind bars, and paid a fine, which everyone agreed was a small price for such a glorious morning's work in defense of freedom. No one said whether the manure ever got cleaned off the highway.

Perhaps someday Tim will get to uphold the farming tradition in this part of the world. Don has worked the land since 1948, owned it since 1963. He is building up the herd again, and he has got some first-calf heifers that set his eyebrows to dancing when he talks about them. Soon they will freshen — have their calves and begin to give milk. With the growing herd, there is plenty of work to be done. Don has been hobbled, and repairs and tidying need attending to.

Tim doesn't seem bashful about tackling the labors, and he seems willing to take his chances with milk — even if the work does smell bad. He is not planning to grow marijuana as a cash crop, as a neighboring farmer was just caught doing. Looking at the story in the morning paper, Tim remarks, "He threw his whole life away." Tim was raised a Mormon and does not drink, smoke, or chew. Today, though, no man or church tells him what to do. He appears a rightful heir to farming's unyielding cruiser-bashers.

Around Stillwater, where once there were farms, now the fields are coming up to cedars, a rot-resistant, pioneering species that thrives in the abandoned cropland and pasture. It seems almost cruel that after the farmers go, the land produces natural material for fence posts.

Enough talk. Time for field work. Tim kisses Mom on the way out.

One realtor said of the residents of Stillwater Township: "They're frightened people." With cause, it appears. The influx of newcomers cannot help but change the township, and Stillwater is not the place it was and probably not the place Joe Connor and Tim Gibbs would like it to be. For the moment, though, it is a reasonable approximation, and laws will be passed to keep the landscape from being remade utterly in the next quarter century as commuters settle in.

Even now, you cannot cut timber off your place without a permit. There is talk of 5-acre zoning. The gravel pit — which, if you think about it, is a strip mine of sorts — is being closed. It was the closing of the gravel pit that led one woman, a long-time resident, to remark, "The working man isn't given a break," and suddenly, quicker than you can say "Karl Marx," there is a whiff of class struggle in the air. How diverse will the paved-driveway crowd be, or will Stillwater someday become one of those towns in which all the residents have clean fingernails?

There was a recent time when people moving to the country had some inchoate, improbably agrarian notion that guided their escape. Today, one senses that simple escape, uncomplicated by ideals of self-sufficiency, is the primary motive of the latest pilgrims. People want a place that is analogous to those idealized images you see of country kitchens: black-ash baskets and herbs hanging from the rafters, the sun illuminating the gingham curtains, an antique pine table with a centerpiece of fresh-cut flowers from the garden. In such a place as that, you know there are no forgotten leftovers growing blue-green and whiskery in the back of the refrigerator. And out of doors, you know that there are no skidders rumbling in the woods, no perfume of cowshit awaft.

Joe Connor talks of a new line of work he has started: "environmentally sensitive development." Is that an oxymoron or a whisper of hope? He tells of a yellow-flowering form of spring beauty that grows in a patch of spring-fed acid soil in Stillwater; it grows nowhere else. Connor wants to see that it continues to survive in the township. Will Don and Tim's cows remain welcome also, or only if the wind takes the smell of them into the hills?